TRUE STORIES
of Elmira, New York
Volume 6

By Diane Janowski & James Hare

This book is a selection of their freelance articles
in the Elmira *Star-Gazette*

True Stories of Elmira, New York, Volume 6

Copyright © 2021 Diane Janowski & James Hare, Elmira, New York

Notice of Rights. All rights reserved by each author. No part of this book may be reproduced or transmitted in any form by any means, electronic, mechanical, photocopying, recording or otherwise, without the prior written permission of the author. For more information on getting permission for reprints and excerpts, contact the author(s).

ISBN: 978-1-950822-20-1

Printed in the United States of America

First Edition

Cover image. Looking northwest from the top of The Park Church. Photograph by Elisha VanAken, circa 1870.

Dedicated to our parents

Robert and Hildegard Janowski

Lovett and Frances Hare

Be sure to look for our other books!

TRUE STORIES
of Elmira, New York

Volumes 1 , 2 , 3, 4, and 5

By James Hare & Diane Janowski

Table of Contents

Frank Buchanan Converse..9
Friends on a River Cruise..13
Lena Gilbert Ford Brown..17
The Elmira Compact..21
Advertising Slogans..25
Tragedy on Main Street..29
Langdon Mansion Part Two...33
Queen City..37
Elmira Driving Park Part Two..41
Elmira and Our Fairs..45
Treaty of Painted Post..49
Ronald Reagan Visited Elmira..53
Notre Dame's 65th Anniversary...57
Elmira College's 1919 Commencement..............................61
Police Chief and Detective Murdered.................................67
Zonta Club in Elmira...73
Crystal Eastman..77
Ross Gilmore Marvin...81
Pentecostal Tabernacle..87
Minstrelsy in Elmira...91
Elmira College's First Ladies...97
Frank E. Bundy...101

A photo of Frank Converse.
Courtesy of Harvard University,
Houghton Library.

FRANK BUCHANAN CONVERSE, BANJO PLAYER
By Diane Janowski

Last year a person asked if I knew anything about an Elmiran named Frank Converse. Instantly, I thought of sneakers. Might sneakers have been invented in Elmira? No, the person said—nothing to do with shoes. Frank Converse was a banjo player. Even better in my mind. Now I got excited, as I play the banjolele, the banjo's little cousin. So, I went off to learn of this Frank Converse. Banjo websites claim Converse to be the most important teacher and promoter of the five-string banjo in the nineteenth century.

The *Pokeepsie Evening Enterprise*, on November 3, 1903, claimed he was the "Father of the Banjo" born in 1837 in Westfield, Massachusetts. The family moved to Elmira in 1841 when Frank was four-years-old. At 16, he left home to become a musician. Frank joined a minstrel company and traveled all over, including London, England. He was known principally as a banjo performer, but he also composed music for the banjo. Some of his songs were "The Vassar Galop," "The Devil's Dance," "Lovely Angelene," and the "Sick Indian Jig."

Frank was the son of Professor of Music, Maxie Manning S. Converse, and Anna Guthrie.

Frank B. Converse was the "King of Stroke Playing" in the 1850s and 60s and also a master of the "guitar style." He wrote at least nine banjo playing books. Banjo scholars will say his "Analytical Banjo Method" has not yet been improved to date.

I found a mention of Frank on the road on April 10, 1860, in the Richmond (Virginia) *Dispatch*, with the advertisement, "Have you heard Frank Converse in his Great BANJO Solo? Many similar ads followed chronologically from all over the United States.

Some papers were very much intrigued by his love life. The Hartford (Connecticut) *Courant* headline on January 30, 1860, read "Marriage of Great Banjoist to a Lady of Wealth." It said, "she was a young and very beautiful lady." Mrs. Harriet Arnot Clark, daughter of Thomas Maxwell of Elmira, was the lucky lady.

The *Courant* went on to say that the pair were "playmates back in Elmira, New York, where the parents of both reside, but as Frank 'never told his love' and joined an itinerant minstrel band. The lady in question accepted the offer of a wealthy New York gentleman three years since. She lived in the enjoyment of unalloyed happiness until some eight months ago when her husband died, leaving her sole heiress to the snug little sum of $150,000 and nary responsibility."

The young widow returned home to Elmira and asked about her childhood friend. Yes, they still liked each other. The trouble was, her family did not want her mixed up with a musician. Her family would not let Frank visit their house. So, secret meetings had to suffice. Opposition from her family eventually brought an elopement for the two to New York City. The Hartford *Courant* continued with, "The facts, as related here, have been confirmed by several who are intimate with the history of both parties, and in whose statements the most implicit confidence can be placed."

In 1884, music stores sold "the celebrated Frank B. Converse Banjo." These banjos are still sold on eBay. He taught the instrument after he ended his career. Banjo enthusiasts claim the decline of the banjo followed soon after the public interest in minstrel performances began to decrease. It is rarely heard on the stage now, even in vaudeville performances, and even the college clubs have lost their old enthusiasm for it.

Frank died at age 66 in Manhattan. His beloved Harriet died one month later. Both are buried in Elmira's Woodlawn Cemetery. Legend has it that Frank has a small headstone because Harriet used most of her money toward philanthropic causes. His stone is also misspelled F. P. C.

On his death, the Elmira *Gazette* cited Frank Converse as "America's best banjo player" on April 18, 1891. The newspaper said his wife, Mrs. Harriet Maxwell Converse, was known as a poet, and an Indianologist (not my term) on April 18, 1891. Frank was also an author of Indian topics.

I didn't know this until I started researching Frank, but banjo musicians from all over the world make pilgrimages to his grave to sit and play their banjos. What an honor!

Converse, Frank B. *Lovely Angelene*, New York, monographic, 1884. Notated Music. https://www.loc.gov/item/

Photo of Henry G. Pohlman in the Elmira *Star-Gazette*, May 15, 1919.

FRIENDS ON A RIVER CRUISE
By Diane Janowski

Every once in a while, you get a defining moment in your life - one that changes everything. In 1911, friends Guthrie and Henry shared one.

School friends Guthrie Knapp, of College Avenue, and Henry Pohlman, of Fulton Street, had such an adventure.

Guthrie loved sports and adventure. At Elmira Free Academy, he was the football team's star player, and also captain and catcher on the baseball team. After graduation, Guthrie maintained his athletic condition by "taking long rambles through the country within a radius of ten miles." (*Star-Gazette* May 20, 1909). In 1909 he found a Native American skeleton with a tomahawk at its side, at the Newtown battlefield. Guthrie collected artifacts of Indian relics and had a fine collection. After graduation, he pursued his career in government. In June 1911, Guthrie returned to Elmira from his job in Panama on a six-week vacation. He was the son of attorney Wilmot Knapp.

Henry Pohlman was the son of German immigrants, Gustave and Augusta Pohlman. He also went to Elmira Free Academy. He loved the river and canoeing and entered many canoe regattas in the early 1900s. Henry also played mandolin in the Knapp Mandolin Orchestra (of today's Knapp Music). Both men would have graduated EFA around 1903-04, but I couldn't find a yearbook that old.

On July 4, 1911, the Elmira *Morning Telegram* reported that Guthrie and Henry were in a 16-foot "Indian Girl" model canoe on the Chemung River to Havre de Grace, Maryland. "Indian Girl" was a canoe built by canoe designer J. H. Rushton in 1902. According to its current website, the "Indian Girl" (still in production) is strong, speedy, graceful, and seaworthy. It was the company's best-selling canoe in the 1910s and 20s. Henry and Guthrie also took a "pup tent and a portable cooking outfit." The plan was to camp each night near a village.

The trip from Elmira to the Chesapeake Bay would be long and arduous – and not for everyone. Luckily, Henry was a member of the Chemung Canoe Camp. He and that group had done the route several years earlier in just eleven days.

So, Henry and Guthrie left Elmira and paddled down the Chemung and Susquehanna Rivers, passing Sayre, Wyalusing, Wilkes-Barre, Sunbury, Harrisburg on July 12, and finally ending at Havre de Grace, Maryland. The river trip took ten days. They had a camera and took some excellent photos, as reported by the *Star-Gazette* on July 19, 1911. None of which were published. They returned home on a train, as Guthrie had a boat to catch from New York City back to Panama on July 29. I found no more mentions of letters written home or to the newspapers from the trip.

Guthrie went back to Panama at the end of July. In 1912 he held a government position there as "secretary to one of the men in charge of constructing the canal." (*Star-Gazette* February 22, 1912)

He gave a personal escort to Mr. & Mrs. J. Sloat Fassett, who were vacationing on the Isthmus. Since Guthrie's appointment, it was the first occasion that he was allowed to express his gratitude to Mr. Fassett for recommending Guthrie for the position.

In 1913 young Guthrie received word that he would be transferred to Manilla in the Philippine Islands to become private secretary to an official in the Bureau of Insular Affairs. In 1915 he became the private secretary to Justice Trent, still in the Philippines. In 1917 he came home to Elmira to enlist with the Elmira troops going to France. I found his World War I draft registration, but no duty records. In 1933 he was assistant to John Hurley of the prohibition office in Washington, DC.

In 1915, Henry Pohlman owned a jewelry store.

Again, I found his World War I draft registration, but no duty records. In 1923, Pohlman was captain of the YMCA's volleyball team. Pohlman continued in the jewelry business and retired in 1954. He and his wife lived on Durland Avenue. The Elmira Country Club still holds the Pohlman Trophy since 1939 – an eighteen-hole tournament named for Henry. Henry died in August 1963 and is buried next to his wife, Ruth.

In Riverdale, Maryland, Guthrie died in 1975 and is buried next to his wife, Frances.

I wonder how many times in their lives Guthrie and Henry thought of their river trip.

Sources:
Star-Gazette (Elmira, New York) 09 Aug 1907, Fri Page 2
Star-Gazette (Elmira, New York) 28 Apr 1914, Tue Page 13
Star-Gazette (Elmira, New York) 20 May 1909, Thu Page 2
Star-Gazette (Elmira, New York) 22 Feb 1912, Thu Page 12
Star-Gazette (Elmira, New York) 13 Oct 1913, Mon Page 3
Star-Gazette (Elmira, New York) 14 Aug 1917, Tue Page 7
Star-Gazette (Elmira, New York) 16 Jan 1923, Tue Page 9

Lena Gilbert Brown Ford. Photo from *Star-Gazette*, November 11, 1964 page 23

LENA GILBERT BROWN FORD
By Diane Janowski

When I went to Elmira College back in the day, if you lived in town, they called you a "Mung." As in Che-mung. Other colleges call their local scholars "townies." I prefer Mung.

A famous Mung from the 1800s was Lena Gilbert Brown Ford. Lena Brown was born in Elmira or Venanda County, Pennsylvania (depending on the source) to James and Antoinette Brown at 246 West Church Street. Father James was listed as an oil manufacturer. By 1880 he was listed as a tobacconist. She attended School #2 (now Booth School), then Elmira College, graduated with a B.A. in 1887, and an M.A. in 1892. Lena flourished in music, acting, and writing.

She married Dr. Harry Hale Ford in Elmira on February 4, 1892. They lived at 422 West Church Street with their son, Walter.

Even after marriage, Lena was popular among the theater-going folks of Elmira. She maintained hopes and aspirations to be an actor. On April 20, 1891, at the Opera House, she played "Iras" in Elmira's hometown production of *Ben Hur*. Many familiar local names were also billed – Mrs. J. S. Fassett, Miss Fannie Rice, A. S. Kingsley, and Lucia Morse. Lena was praised for her "trained elocutionist interpretation." However, her performance was "marred by loud talking behind the curtains." After the performance, she received a big basket of flowers. After the three-night engagement in Elmira, Lena received an invitation to continue with the troupe at Watertown's next performance. The local production netted 45% to the producers and 45% (about $750) given to the benefit of the Anchorage Home (for way-ward girls) on College Avenue. The last 10% went to the Opera House and for expenses.

The marriage ended in divorce, and Lena took her mother and son to Italy and France. In 1902 they settled in London. Lena wrote weekly articles for the Anglo-American newspaper. From this, she expanded to other publications in both prose and verse.

In WWI, she opened her home to convalescing soldiers and took care of them. In 1914 she collaborated with Ivor Novello and wrote the lyrics to "Till the Boys Come Home." In 1915 the song was re-released as "Keep the Home-Fires Burning." It was the first significant success for Novello and Lena's only success. The song was a colossal hit first in Europe, then in the U.S.

Two German bombs dropped from a dirigible struck Lena's home in Warrington Crescent, London, on March 7, 1918. Lena, age 58, and her 31-year old disabled son Walter instantly died. Mrs. Brown survived. Lena and son Walter were buried in the Willesden cemetery in North London.

Lena has a memorial fireplace in Elmira College's Hamilton Hall with the inscription: Lena Gilbert Ford Brown, Class of 1887, "Keep the Home Fires Burning."

Some lines from the song....

> *Keep the Home Fires burning*
> *While your hearts are yearning*
> *Though your lads are far away*
> *They dream of home*
> *There's a silver lining*
> *Through the dark cloud shining*
> *Turn the dark cloud inside out*
> *Till the boys come Home*

Sources:

Star-Gazette (Elmira, New York) April 22, 1891, Wed Page 5
Chemung Historical Journal March 1965
Wikipedia.com

Zebulon Brockway, Fusion mayoral candidate, 1905. He was the former superindentent of the Elmira Reformatory. This photo from June 1895. *Star-Gazette* (Elmira, New York)
05 Apr 1995, Wed Page 7

ELMIRA COMPACT – OR, SPEAKING OF VOTER FRAUD
By Diane Janowski

I may be the only person who knows what the "Elmira Compact" was, although there was a time in the early 1900s when the whole country read about it in their local newspapers.

The story starts well before 1905, when "corrupt practices" were discovered at local elections. Votes were bought and sold in the olden times. Men, I say "men" because women were not yet allowed to vote, could make a good day's work and dinner between visiting ALL the voting stations. Men of this nature were called "floaters."

In Elmira elections, some candidates paid with food like sandwiches or hamburgers, some paid cash, some settled in beer and whiskey at local saloons. Certain persons of our community voted frequently and often, as the saying goes. No proof of identity was needed; folks used made-up names and made-up addresses.

Jacob Sloat Fassett had had enough in 1905 and, along with John B. Stanchfield while playing golf at the Elmira Country Club, discussed money-spending for elections, and both agreed that it would be a good thing if it could be eliminated. They sat down and penned the "famous" Elmira Compact.

In short, the Elmira Compact promised four things.
1. Candidates could only spend $40 on their campaigns per election district
2. No money could change hands before or during the election process to purchase or influence votes
3. Bribery will result in the arrest, prosecution, and conviction of those committing the offense

4. Rewards of $100 to any person offering information on election offenses

Signed by J.S. Fassett, chairman of Republican Party, and W.H. Lovell, chairman of Democratic Party, October 5, 1905

The *Star-Gazette* editor was in favor of the Compact, knowing that local politics were not "absolutely pure," but instead, it would make "make things better and keep things better."

Fassett and Stanchfield spoke at both Republican and Democratic headquarters in Elmira. Somehow both parties agreed to clean campaigning and would limit their expenditures to $25 for each city district and $40 for each county district. The idea caught on in Ithaca, Norwich, Schoharie, Middletown, Cobleskill, Columbia County, and Ogdensburg.

The 1905 mayoral election in Elmira had one Fusion candidate as both parties shared Zebulon Brockway. Brockway easily won. Attorneys and detectives had been stationed in each voting district "not in the anticipation of crime, but in the interest of legal and clean elections." The election was not contested or recounted. Brockway was satisfied, but nobody else was. Some enterprising voters wanted cash, drinks, or food to which they had become accustomed.

"Elmira had in 1905, the cleanest, most decent, and most satisfactory city election in two decades." On November 17, 1906, Fassett wrote to the Elmira *Gazette* editor and said, "[the last] election was free and clean of bribery, so far as I know. The thing that did happen; that scores and scores of men came to the polls demanded pay, and when payment was refused, they went home without voting. In one election district, there were about 100, in other districts 40 to 50." He also went on to suggest that Elmira advocate a "head tax on all male citizens over 21 years of age, which tax should be remitted upon proof that a man voted at the next election.

He suggested a tax of $10 or $20.

The Elmira Compact idea lasted until 1907, when Fassett could no longer agree with the concept as he believed "the Democrats broke the compact." On the other hand, John Moore of the Elmira *Telegram* emphatically declared that "both parties had broken the Compact." The Compact had given the appearance of "a good business-like government." Elmirans missed our usual fighting and bickering, and so in the next election Democrat, Daniel Sheehan won and lasted for the next six years.

And here we are.

Sources:

Star-Gazette (Elmira, New York)26 Oct 1906, Fri Page 8
Star-Gazette (Elmira, New York) 24 Sep 1906, Mon Page 4
Star-Gazette (Elmira, New York) 28 Sep 1906, Fri Page 4
Star-Gazette (Elmira, New York) 03 Oct 1906, Wed Page 6
Star-Gazette (Elmira, New York) 25 Jul 1901, Thu Page 4
Star-Gazette (Elmira, New York) 17 Nov 1906, Sat Page 7
Star-Gazette (Elmira, New York) 29 Sep 1908, Tue page 6
Star-Gazette (Elmira, New York) 27 Jun 1939, Tue Page 58

Image from the *Star-Gazette* October 11, 1906 page 4

Image from the *Star-Gazette* Feb 22, 1950 page 4

ADVERTISING SLOGANS FROM ELMIRA'S PAST
By Diane Janowski

Slogans for advertised products became common around 1890. They made the reader remember a product or concept. Printed advertisements in Elmira in the late 19th and early 20th centuries were simple and to the point.

In 1863 the Farmers and Citizens Dining Saloon at 171 Water Street advertised "Warm Food at All Hours. Bartering was OK at O. B. Northrup Boots and Shoes at 152 Water Street. O. B. said, "Produce Taken in Exchange for Goods." The Elmira Steam Bakery at 421 Railroad Avenue baked, "Crackers, A Specialty."

In 1884 Clay Holmes was the Southern Tier Manufacturing Company owner, which produced many fine medicinal products including, Hale's Toothache Drops, Hale's Corn Drops, Hale's Honey of Horehound and Tar, and Hale's Worm Candy. Holmes claimed his medicines were "pleasant, effective, and harmless." His laboratory was at 122 Lake Street.

In 1885 the Caputoleum Company at the corner of Main and Water Streets advertised "Caputoleum," a hair elixir guaranteed to "Restore Hair to Bald Heads.

George Elmendorf of Riverside Avenue manufactured "Elmendorf's Pine Tar Gum" in 1901, claiming it cured "Colds, Hay fever, the Grippe, Asthma, and keeps away Worms and other diseases."

Elmirans who ate too much in 1908 could check-in to the Bishop Health Institute at 118 West Second Street for their "Treatment for Overfatness." It was infallible. They also cured rheumatism and gout with their "Hydro-Electric Bath Treatment."

A 1909 ad for Mrs. Frances Kellogg's Hair Dressing Parlor read, "If you have Dandruff, see Mrs. Kellogg."

In 1912, Flynn's Palace Bath Rooms in the Robinson Building on Lake Street specialized in "Turkish, Roman, Russian, and Plain Baths," and every Friday was Ladies Day.

During the 1918 flu epidemic, several stores advertised "Influenza Germ Killer – Disinfect Air Passages with Smo-ko Cigarettes – A few puffs and – goodbye Grippe. The smoke you inhale carries a healing and medicating disinfectant which penetrates the air passage that cannot be reached any other way."

After work or school in 1936, you could "Treat Yourself to Schmick's Golden Vanilla Ice Cream" at 534 Broadway. And don't forget Elmira's own Frozen Sunshine from Hygeia Ice Cream with flavors like Parker House, Nesselrode, Burnt Almond, and Pineapple Marshmallow.

Elmira had at least two businesses with dual purposes. In 1931, Harry W. Honan had the right idea for solving one or two problems with his business ad for "ambulance and Funeral Director." Another store with a dual purpose was the Elmira Pioneer Furniture and Undertaking Establishment at East Water and State Streets in 1901.

Carpenter's Diner had a sense of humor with their slogan "We Seat 500 People – 50 At A Time."

In 1946 if you had a lovely home but also had pests, you called the Abalene Pest Control because they said, "We Kill or Exterminate Rats, Mice, Roaches, and Bedbugs with our cyanide fumigation method."

For sweethearts, carloads of teenagers, and adults of all ages, the Elmira Drive-In Theater on Route 352 was "Air Conditioned by Nature." In August 1960, they showed an excellent double feature of *The Giant Gila Monster* and *The Killer Shrews*.

Robinson Airlines out of the Chemung County Airport in the 1950s offered "Speed, Comfort, and Low Fares" with daily flights to exotic locales like Erie, Pennsylvania, for $9.30. Buffalo for $5.00. Washington DC for $14.40. and Pittsburgh for $13.80.

The history of American advertising is the history of American life. It follows our strengths and weaknesses.

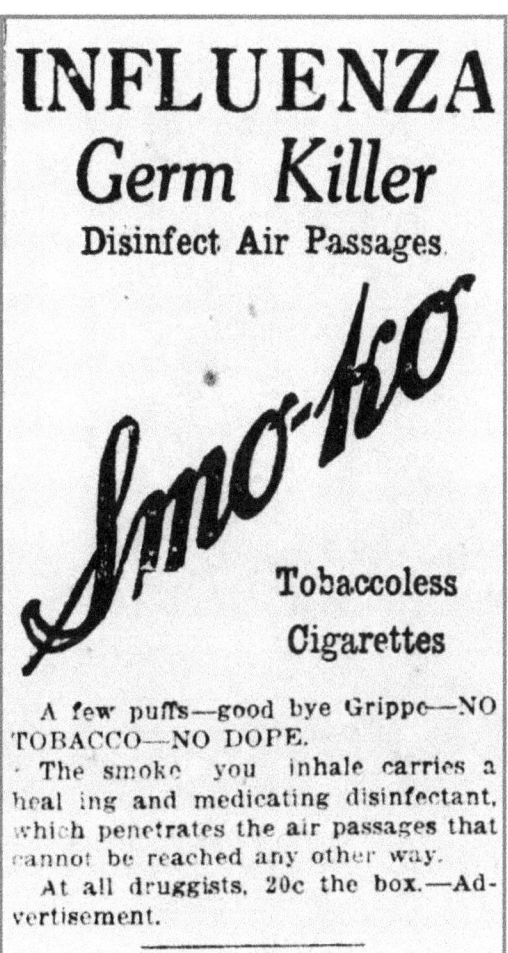

Image from the *Star-Gazette* November 1, 1918 page 5

This photo, taken from the roof of a building across the street from the cave-in, shows how traffic was held up at Main and Water Streets during the work of rescue. Crowds were kept clear of danger zone by efficient police cordon.

Star-Gazette June 14, 1930 page 3

TRAGEDY ON MAIN STREET
By Diane Janowski

The *Star-Gazette* reported some bad news.

It was Friday the 13th, June 1930. Rush hour traffic was heavy downtown when a roar echoed through the streets at 4:55 pm. A wooden walkway on Main Street between the Gorton Coy building and Iszard's department store collapsed into a 15-foot hole. The crashing walkway took with it 24 pedestrians. A child died instantly. Little Maria Smolka, age 11, of Elmira Heights, died on the spot. Other people suffered broken legs, arms, skulls, collarbones, fractured ribs, and many lacerations, abrasions, contusions, concussions, sprains, shock, lots of blood. Screaming and suffering followed the catastrophe. An estimated 200 were in the near vicinity.

Sisters Effie Corey and Ella Warner were amongst the worst of the victims. Effie died three days later of a fractured skull.

Elmira police officer Edward Carroll who was minding the crosswalk, accounted that he heard the "creaking of timbers, and saw many people falling into the hole at the south end." Planks fell on people and knocked them into the pit. Heavy timbers and steel rods pinned folks in the pit.

The wooden walkway was a tunnel-like structure built over the sidewalk. It was built to protect walkers from falling objects at the new Gorton Coy building's construction site. Workers had piled a large quantity of rebar or reinforcing steel rods on top of the enclosure, adding to its weight. The weight of the steel and the walkers proved too much for the structure to withstand. The vibration of the heavy traffic and incessant trolleys did not help the matter, either.

The construction company claimed that the building was being constructed on a "former swamp" and filled in with inadequate undersoil.

Rescue crews worked well into the night to ensure no other bodies had been buried in the wreckage. The sirens from police, fire, ambulances, and the pounding of axes and shouts of rescuers made it challenging to hear. Fire Chief Espey said it was a pathetic sight to see the maimed victims.

It was difficult to see what was going on because of the large cloud of cement dust and dirt in the air. Construction workers and passersby jumped into action before the first responders arrived. Three fire companies came.

Three ambulances lined up behind Iszard's department store. Radio stations broadcasted an immediate call for doctors and nurses over the local radio airwaves. Twenty-five arrived almost instantly. Six ministers also came. Rescuers took injured folks to the back rooms of Iszard's store and the Sheeley brothers' flower shop for triage. The ambulances ferried the injured to St. Josephs and Arnot Ogden hospitals as quickly as possible. Franklin Crayton, who owned a confectionary store at 110 North Main Street, began brewing coffee and making sandwiches for all the rescuers and volunteers at the scene.

Little Maria was downtown that afternoon (as she was most afternoons) to sell candy door-to-door to business people. She did not show up for her piano lesson at 7:30 pm, and her parents got worried. They knew there had been a problem in Elmira. Out of desperation, they called the Arnot-Odgen hospital and were told to come down. Yes, it was their daughter. Maria was in the fifth grade at School One in Elmira Heights.

In September 1930, four civil lawsuits against Lowman Construction combined as the trial began. Before the trial, this first action settled out of court and awarded the plaintiff a combined $62,000. Additional actions began on September 12, granted $7,500 for one defendant. The plaintiff appealed in Supreme Court, asking for $25,000. Effie Corey's estate received $3,000 out of court on September 19. Another victim received $4,000 on October 3. Plaintiffs filed several more actions. Some went to trial. I did not find the settlement of Maria Smolka.

The Gorton Coy opened for business on Friday, March 13, 1931.

Star-Gazette June 14, 1930 page 2

Sources

Star-Gazette (Elmira, New York) June 14, 1930, Sat Page 2
Star-Gazette (Elmira, New York) June 14, 1930, Sat Page 3

The north side of the Langdon home showing the early house with the new house and the circular driveway. *Star-Gazette* photo.

LANGDON MANSION PART 2
By Diane Janowski

I wrote about the demise of the Langdon home in the November 3, 2017 edition of the *Star-Gazette*. I have some more to report.

Before COVID, I had coffee with a group of friends every Friday morning at Steve Seaberg's State Farm insurance office in Langdon Plaza. Sometimes we wondered which part of the Langdon Mansion we were sitting in. After a sleepless night last month with a lot of thinking, I got up to find a floor plan of the old mansion and overlay it on today's Langdon Plaza to see what was what.

The Langdon Mansion is well documented by stereographic views dating from 1878-1880. The surviving furniture and decorative accessories are preserved at the Chemung County Historical Society and Quarry Farm, east of Elmira.

Jervis was born in 1809 in Vernon, New York. Moved to Elmira in 1845 from Millport with his wife, Olivia. Jervis was interested in the lumber industry and made much money in his endeavors. By 1860 the family had enormous wealth, from lumber and then anthracite coal.

The family had three children, Olivia, who later married Samuel Clemens, our Mark Twain, Charles, and Susan. The Langdon home had two servants in 1860, Mary Lewis and Catherine Mahon, both from Ireland.

The family lived in several Elmira locations before purchasing a lot in 1862 near Main and Church streets owned by Anson Ely. In 1865 Jervis bought the corner lot that had a "modest but elegant" Greek Revival residence. As the house was not big enough, Jervis built an addition and remodeled the whole place as Italianate. Remodeled is the word they used. In my opinion, they built a whole big new house attached to the older smaller house. The result was a three-story mansion – exceptional for Elmira and filled with the latest fashionable furniture. An architect adorned the brownstone home with a pedimented pavilion in front, bays on both sides, and a telescoping arrangement of wings. Around the back were a carriage house and a greenhouse. The architect was likely Andrew J. Warner of Rochester. Warner was known for his wide porches that featured a central arch opening.

The inside of the house was commissioned to Pottier and Stymus, a new furniture and design firm in New York City, who were to do the cabinets, decorating, painting, carpets, curtains, and handmade wood furniture. The firm had notable clients. The Langdon drawing-room was the largest and most elaborate of all the rooms. The furniture was ebonized cherry embellished with gilt-bronze mounts and medallions. Pottier & Stymus borrowed forms from aristocratic French furniture. The decorators demonstrated Langdon's good taste. In later years after Jervis died, Olivia continued to use Pottier & Stymus to create new furniture suites for several bedrooms.

Olivia continued to live at 303 North Main Street until she died in 1890. The house went to son Charles. Charles and his wife Ida made changes in 1890.

The house was demolished in 1939, and Langdon Plaza opened in 1940.

So, back to the 1903 floor plan and today's layout, if you visit Steve Seaberg's office in Langdon Plaza, please note that you are standing in the Langdon kitchen.

For lots more information about this subject, please see:
Walter G. Ritchies "The Jervis Langdon Residence in Elmira, New York." Mark Twain Journal 56, no. 1 (2018): 72-85.
http://www.jstor.org/stable/45173256.

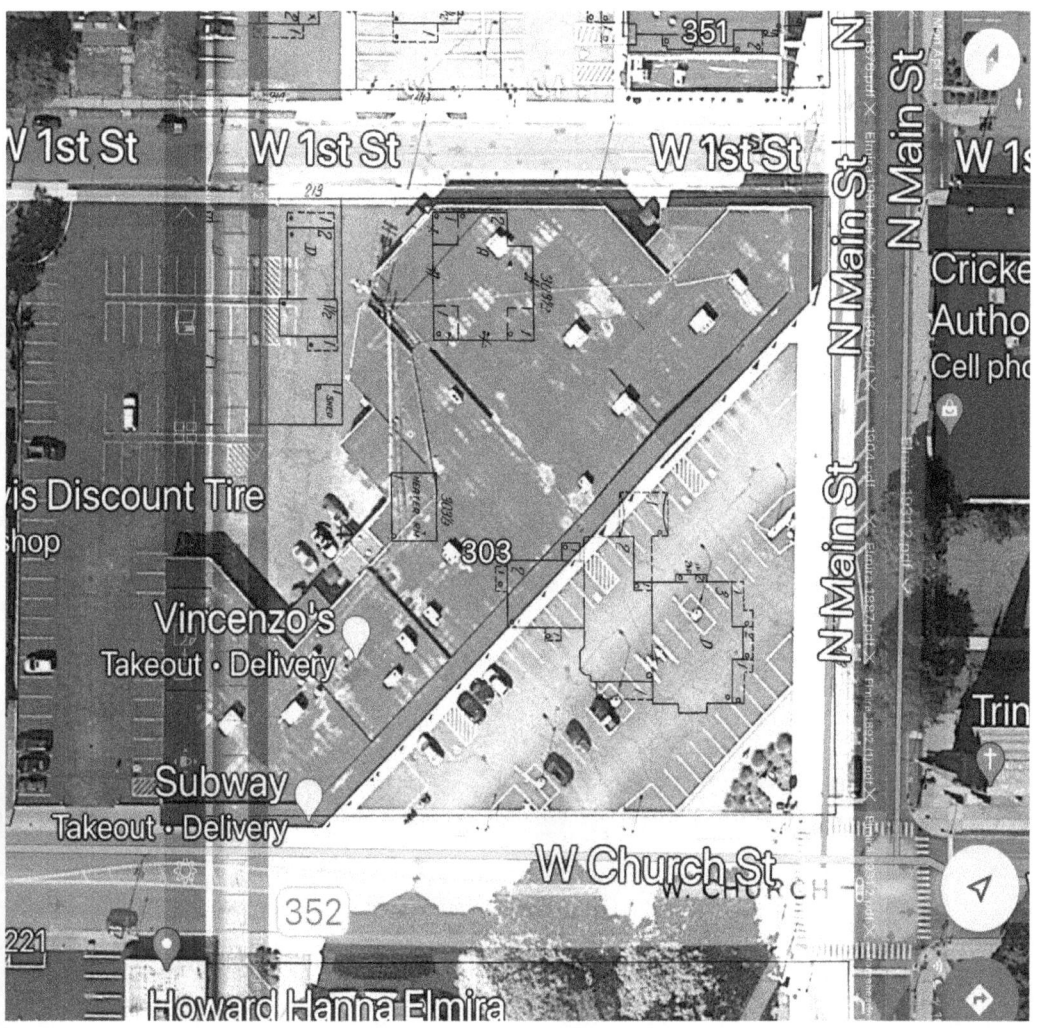

I overlayed the Langdon floorplan from the 1903 Sanborn map with a current Google map.

Cover image of *Harper's New York and Erie Railroad Guide*.

HOW ELMIRA GOT TO BE KNOWN AS THE QUEEN CITY
By Diane Janowski

"Elmira is the Queen City along New York and Erie Railroad, and is a good specimen of the towns that seem to exhale from the American soil..." This statement was penned by William MacLeod in 1851 in *Harper's New York and Erie Railroad Guide*. It was only two years prior, in 1849, that the railroad had arrived in Elmira.

To promote this brand new rail line through New York to travelers, Harper's magazine sent a team to highlight the route - including travel writer William MacLeod to report on the sights along the way. MacLeod described Elmira, "...Situated on the north bank of the Chemung, we enter its streets by a covered bridge of wood. The traveler, as he skirts along its suburbs to its busy station in the west end, and then passes to his hotel through those compact streets, crowded with business and intersected by a canal..."

He goes on to explain Elmira's early history and importance. The first Erie station was described as extensive with an agent's office, freight houses, and a large engine house with a turn-table. Other local towns mentioned in the Guide are Waverly, Chemung, Wellsburg, Horseheads, Big Flats, and Corning.

The craze for railroads had come in the summer of 1831 with the need for a business route through the Southern Tier of New York – the northern route being the Erie Canal. New York City had the New York & Harlem railroad that opened in stages between 1832 and 1852.

At the beginning of 1832 there were only 44 miles of railroad operating upstate, 15 miles of the Mohawk & Hudson Railroad, and 29 miles of the Ithaca & Owego Railroad.

The first public expression for the southern route was during a meeting in Monticello on July 29, 1831, with the plan that many small railroad companies that would join at county borders. Subsequent meetings occurred at Jamestown, Angelica and Owego.

Delegates from all related counties converged on this meeting in Owego. During the meeting, a messenger delivered a note suggesting that the railroad be built as a whole by one company, and not in sections by many small companies. After a long struggle, the committee resolved that one railroad would operate the line from Lake Erie to the Hudson River and connect with railroads already chartered, with a capital of $5,000,000.

They jokingly, at the time, said it might be possible to go from Buffalo to New York City in 24 hours.

The railroad's construction began in 1835 at Deposit in Broome County. The first completed section was between Piermont and Goshen in 1841, Goshen to Middletown in 1843, to Port Jervis in 1848, to Elmira in 1849, to Corning in 1850, and finally terminating in Dunkirk in 1851. The first express train through on the entire line from Dunkirk to New York was on May 19, 1851. It took only 17 hours.

It was then that Harpers commissioned the *Railroad Guide* and labeled Elmira the "Queen City." Elmirans embraced their new nickname, and over the years many businesses and organizations have used it for their promotion, such as: Queen City Palace Hotel, Queen City Sewer Pipes, Queen City Flower Store, Queen City Hat Cleaning Shop, Queen City Paper. The last remaining use is by the Queen City Elks Lodge on Benjamin Street.

An artist from Harper's magazine climbed East Hill and sketched Elmira in 1851.

Harper's New York and Erie Railroad Guide has recently been reprinted in its original form with beautiful illustrations and is available at Chemung-History.com

The entrance to the Elmira Driving Park at Eldridge Park, 1875. The image is not credited, but I believe this to be the work of local photographer Elisha VanAken. Image in the collection of the author.

ELMIRA DRIVING PARK PART 2
By Diane Janowski

I wrote about the horse "American Girl" dying at the Elmira Driving Park in a *Star-Gazette* article dated April 1, 2015. In addition, Jim Hare has written about the Wilcox and Maple Avenue Driving Parks. I recently acquired a new photograph to my collection, so I want to add some more to the subject.

To recap a little of that story - Elmira has had three driving parks in its history. A "driving park" was an area with a racetrack for harness racing.

The Elmira *Daily Advertiser* reported that on May 17, 1867, Elmira opened its first driving park on the property of Dr. E. Eldridge on the southside of the river, along what is today's Hudson Street. Its prime mover was Colonel Fortis Wilcox, former hotel landlord of the Delevan House in Elmira. Wilcox spent many months preparing the ground and designing a driving park. He created a place of "elegant and recreative resort." Wilcox also added a hotel – a place where "pleasure riders may rest." It was a unique wooden structure. It is a great ornament to the taste and excellent arrangement of the park itself."

A grand opening was held on May 29 with a cavalcade of horses with the young stallion "Henry Clay" in the lead. Next came a show of 4-year-olds, then a presentation of mares, horses, and stallions of all ages. Finally, a sweepstakes event included all ages of horses. Admission was 25¢ for men; ladies were free.

Eight years later, in 1875, a charter was amended in Albany for Elmira's second driving park – this time at Eldridge Park. I have a new-to-me photograph of this park. Workers built grandstands and refreshment booths just to the east of Grand Central Avenue, now known as Lake Welmer, or more affectionately "the swamp." A luxurious hotel also graced the property. Its proximity to the New York State Fairgrounds (at this time - east of Eldridge Park) was also a significant draw. Yes, Elmira hosted the New York state fair nine times between 1855 and 1889.

By August 1875, all the buildings had been finished, except for some finishing touches on the grandstand."

On September 23, 1875, the *Daily Advertiser* reported the park as having "a magnificent new half-mile track, even more, expansive than the track in Rochester, with splendid stretches and easy turns, with the most commodious stables for horses. The driving park has been built by a company of wealthy and sport-loving citizens of Elmira. It has been supplied with a first-rate hotel and a grandstand.

The driving park opened during the New York State Fair, and Elmira streetcars ran directly to each from downtown every fifteen minutes. From what I can tell, the State Fair was more like a business expo of today.

Many local businesses showcased their products. Companies such as J. M. Robinson showed furniture, Simon Sayles & Co with their roasted coffee, Greener's showed their grand pianos, and Smith & Lawrence showed their candy. Other booths were picture frames, dry goods, saddles, and hardware. The most popular booth of the fair was Billing's and Brooks' burglar alarms. It was estimated that there were 20,000 visitors to Elmira on September 30, 1875.

The grand opening of the park enjoyed much press the week before. Fifty-one horses came from all over the United States and were scheduled to run that weekend, including the ill-fated "American Girl," who unfortunately died during a race on October 2.

There were many fast horses locally, but racing popularity dwindled quite quickly. The last official race at Eldridge Park was about 1880

– five years after it opened. This track was used in 1883 when Buffalo Bill brought his Wild West show to Elmira during the New York State Fair.

The grounds reverted to a swamp after the abandonment of the racetrack and had turned into a haven for gypsies and squatters. Today a paved path leads from Eldridge Park to Lake Street, home to turtles, herons, kingfishers, and muskrats. Halfway through, visitors can take the northern trail along the remains of the Chemung Canal.

The third driving park – the Maple Avenue driving park (today's Dunn Field area) opened in 1886 and lasted until 1910. Please see Jim Hare's article in the *Star-Gazette* for more info – June 28, 2020.

Sources
Elmira *Daily Advertiser* May 17, 1867, page 1
Ithaca *Daily Journal* April 13, 1875 page 1
Elmira *Daily Advertiser* August 9, 1875, Page 2, Image 2
Elmira *Daily Advertiser* September 25, 1875, Page 4, Image 4
Elmira *Daily Advertiser* September 25, 1875, Page 4, Image 4
Elmira *Daily Advertiser* September 30, 1875
https://wskg.org/history/elmira-fair-grounds-1889-tbt/

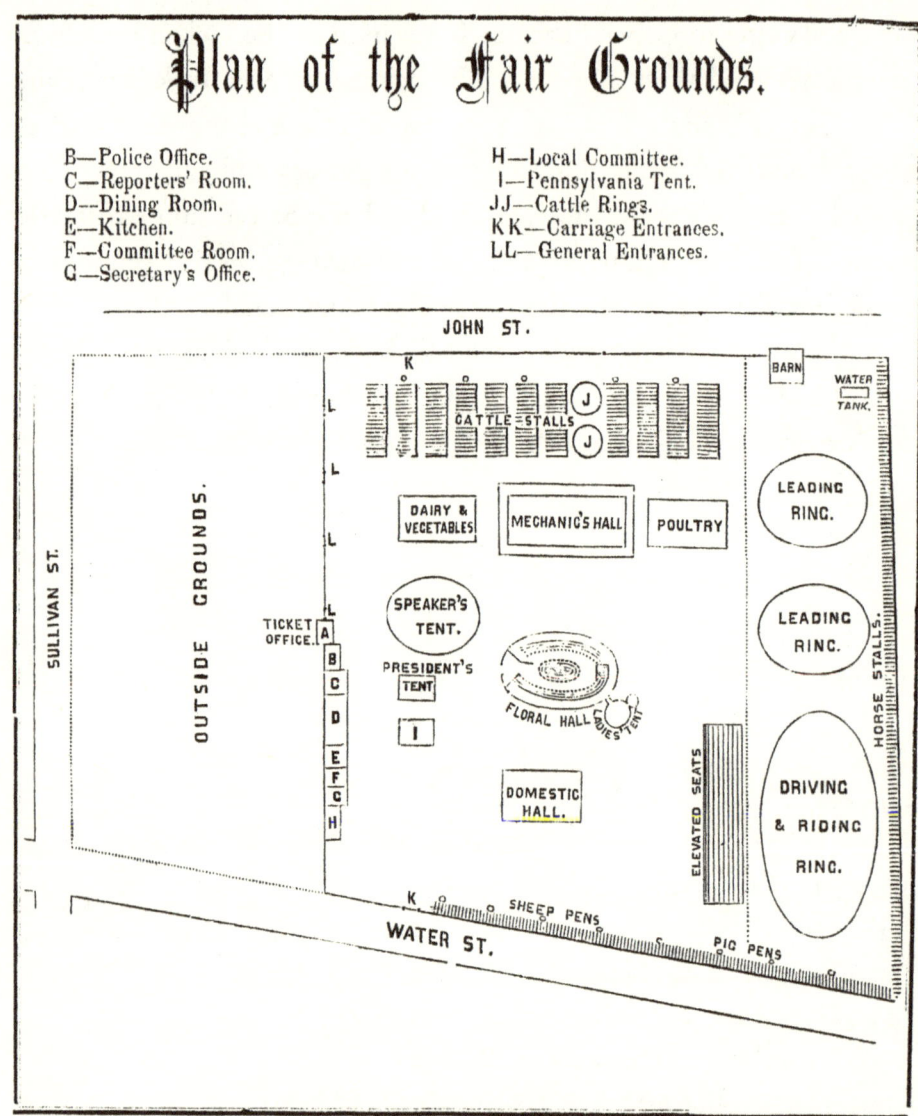

STATE FAIR—This map is from the 1855 Directory for "the use of Citizens and Strangers" at the State Fair. The Fairgrounds were between John St., and Water St., east of Sullivan, location of the present Kennedy Valve Co.

ELMIRA AND OUR FAIRS
By Diane Janowski

Last year because of COVID, there was no Chemung County fair, and I was forced to make my sausage and pepper sandwich at home. This year I am hoping to eat my sandwich near the sound of the demo derby.

The Chemung County fair began as a showcase for local agricultural businesses in 1842. Animals and garden products, and tools were a big draw. Lapses in the "sometimes annual" county fairs occurred, and a few years were missed.

The New York State Fair was also held in Elmira seven times - 1855, 1860, 1869, 1872, 1875,1878, 1883. Eventually, Syracuse became the official home of the state fair. Our earliest fairs were held in Horseheads, then some were held east of Eldridge Park, some on the grounds of today's Kennedy Valve property, and a least one was held at the Maple Avenue driving park. The date I know for sure was the 1875 fair held east of Eldridge Park. Also, three interstate fairs between New York and Pennsylvania were held at the Maple Avenue driving park in 1889, 1890, and 1891.

The early state fairs always opened with an address and a ball. The ball was held inside the Floral Hall, and it was the most prominent social event of the year. Women and men wore their best "dress to impress clothes." Country and city folk came from all around. Hotels were full and businesses boomed while the fair was going on.

An agricultural society began in our county in 1842. The first and foremost action was to "wage a war of extermination against our common enemy, the Canadian Thistle." Twice a year, officials had to "cut the noxious weed on each side of the highways." I know for a fact that we never did eradicate that pest, and they still grow every year.

A few county fairs were held under this society. The 1842 fair had divisions in horses, cattle, swine, heifers, cheese, grain crops, root crops, fruit, silk, and agricultural implements. The society reorganized in 1853. Again, several county fairs were held. The Elmira Farmers' Club began in 1869 and it took over the events.

Politics were essential to our early county fairs. It was the best and easiest way for candidates to meet and greet the public in one central place. Many folks came to town just to hear their opinions.

The State Fair's last visit to Elmira was in 1883. The fairgrounds had a Floral Hall, several leading rings for horses, a driving ring for horses, a poultry barn, a mechanic's hall. Also, a speaker's tent, the president's tent, and cattle stalls. According to the brochure's map, some smart person designed the grandstand to be built next to the pig pens.

The official county fairgrounds moved to its present location in 1892 with 35 acres of the former Shoot farm. We have loved and supported the fair every year.

Our fairground hosts numerous animal shows, festivals, and exhibits. 2021 marks the 179th Chemung County Fair. There is barn space for 400 horses and a quarter-mile horse racetrack. Mmm, funnel cakes, and corn dogs are calling my name.

Sources:
https://wskg.org/history/elmira-fair-grounds-1889-tbt/
Towner, Ausburn *History of Chemung County 1892*
Byrne, Thomas *Chemung County 1976*

August 21, 1946 harness racing at the Chemung County Fairgrounds. Image courtesy of the *Star-Gazette*.

The Treaty of Painted Post monument on East Market Street.

ELMIRA HISTORY: BEHIND THE TREATY OF PAINTED POST MONUMENT
by James Hare

"I bet a lot of people go by here every day and don't know what this is all about," said Rep. Amory Houghton on July 4, 1991.

He was attending a commemoration of the signing of the Treaty of Painted Post of 1791, and "pointing to the granite and bronze monument placed inconspicuously in the lawn behind the Chemung County Courthouse near the corner of Market and Lake streets," according to the Corning *Leader*.

The treaty was drawn up and signed at Newtown (Elmira) by Colonel Timothy Pickering, representing the United States government, and by the chiefs of the Six Iroquois Nations. Some accounts say that from 1,500 to 1,800 Indians were present, camping along the river trail where Water Street now runs from Sullivan Street to the western border of the city. The treaty signed that day was never ratified by the United States Senate, and it appears no copies exist, but it proved to be a complete success because it stopped all hostilities between the white settlers and the Indians.

The granite and bronze monument sits behind the Chemung County Courthouse.

The reason for the ceremony taking place in Newtown and not Painted Post was, in the words of Colonel Pickering, "the waters of the Tioga (Chemung) River are so low that the provisions and stores can be got up no farther than Newtown Point about 20 miles from the place where of course the Treaty will be held."

Pickering would end up persuading the chiefs to meet him at Newtown.

In 1927, the current monument was dedicated before 1,000 people. Mayor David M. Heller said, "This place was Newtown, then a small and seemingly insignificant settlement. Today it is Elmira, a flourishing city. Newtown was, Elmira is, and anything which was important to Newtown in 1791 is of importance to Elmira in 1927."

Mayor Heller went on to say, "… Memorials are more or less the product of sentiment …let us resolve that an interest in all things which pertain to our city shall be strengthened and kept alive."

As mayor at the 1991 commemoration, I could do no better than to paraphrase and quote my predecessor.

Today, in our nation, we have a discussion ongoing about monuments. At the 1927 ceremony, Chief Walter Kennedy, clerk of the Seneca Indians on the Salamanca Reservation, gave an "inspiring address." It seems relevant to quote at length what he said.

"I feel greatly and highly honored in being invited to participate in the dedication commemorating one of the treaties made between the United States on the one part and the Six Nations of Indians, so called, on the other part; one of the Nations of which I happened to be a descendant, that is the Seneca Nation, who at one time owned this same land on which your beautiful city of Elmira is now located.

"In the first place, we Indians cannot understand why the white man claimed this country by right of discovery, when it was already inhabited by a race of people; the aboriginal inhabitants surely must have some right to this country by right of prior possession. If the aboriginal inhabitants of this continent were the savage, ferocious, blood-thirsty, wild men that your school books have pictured him to be, he would never have allowed the white men to land on the shores of the North American continent. But, I am very proud to say, it was otherwise. Instead of being the savage, blood-thirsty wild men they were the most

hospitable race of people inhabiting the face of the globe.

"Prior to 1776, the Indian disputed the right of Great Britain to the soil of this country; he disputed the right of France to the soil of this country, and was continually at war with these nations over the question. After the thirteen colonies sought to free themselves from the tyrannical despotism of Great Britain, in which they succeeded, the Six Nations of Indians assembled in council and appointed a commission consisting of one member from each Nation to go to General George Washington and ask what the status of the Six Nations would be. General Washington, replying to this question said, 'In so far as you gave aid and succor to Great Britain in this late struggle, you must emigrate and go to British soil.'

"The Seneca Nation assembled in council and appointed a commission ... to say to General Washington, We Indians, own this country. King George had no right to cede this country to you. We declare a war, a war of extermination. When you conquer us, then we will emigrate, otherwise we will stay here.

"This great state of New York was in favor of driving the remnants of the Six Nations from their home lands, so was General Washington, but through the influence of General Schuyler, who argued that it would be cheaper to make treaties with us and purchase these lands from the Indians than to cause bloodshed, treaties were made, one of which we are now commemorating.

"My fondest hope and dearest wish is, that some day we Indians will be treated like human beings by these great United States of America, the most enlightened and humane nation in the world"

(Star-Gazette, July 5, 1927).

The chief's sentiments offer perspective on the debate about the meaning and purpose of monuments. With regard to the treaty, former County Historian J. Arthur Kieffer commented in the *Chemung Valley Reporter* on June 20, 1991, "though no copy of the treaty can be found in federal files, Pickering's journals and other documents prove that the treaty existed."

THE TIME RONALD REAGAN VISITED ELMIRA
by James Hare

John Massey remembers clearly his meeting Ronald Reagan, the 40th president of the United States. However, the meeting took place 22 years before Reagan entered the Oval Office, and John, now 77, was just 15 years of age.

Reagan was in Elmira headlining the program for the second annual kickoff dinner launching the United Community Chest-Red Cross Campaign on October 2, 1958.

The October 3, 1958 *Star-Gazette* reported, "The United Community Chest - Red Cross Campaign's kickoff dinner last night started with a real symbol of the benefits of the campaign — and one that drew the admiration of the crowd. The five-Scout color guard opening the program was composed of members of one family, the children of Mr. and Mrs. John Massey of 512 Balsam Street."

The paper went on to note that "in addition to the five children ... Mrs. Massey (Helen) serves as a den mother with Pack 15 of the Centenary Church, where her son Dwight, 9, is a Cub Scout. Mr. Massey is a committeeman for Troop 48 of the Coburn School where his son James, 11, is a second class Boy Scout and John, 15, is an Explorer Scout and junior assistant leader. Ten-year-old Barbara is a Girl Scout with Troop 91 of the Hardy School and Debra, 7, is a Brownie with the Hardy School Troop. Mrs. Massey said that, 'the oldest one started it and the others wanted to follow. They enjoy it and we always know where they are ...' John proudly notes that they were the Scouting Family of the Year for 1958.

Ronald Reagan stopped in Elmira in October of 1958.

Meeting Reagan was a big surprise, as the youngsters were not told until shortly before the event that he would be present. John recalls that they knew him from the General Electric Theater on television. He said Reagan was a "real nice man, very polite and looked like he did on black and white TV."

Reagan spent a full day in Elmira. He arrived that Thursday morning and held a press conference at the Mark Twain Hotel at 11:30 a.m. He then appeared at the General Electric Company luncheon at the hotel and from there went to the Elmira Foundries (formerly on Thurston Street) to tour the plant. At 3:45, he spoke to approximately 300 students at Elmira College and attended a reception for agency officials before going to the kickoff dinner.

The United Community Chest/Red Cross Campaign hoped to raise $462,689. J. Lawrence Kolb, the drive chairman, stated that the goal was a "little more" that the amount asked for last year, "but is $26,000 more than was raised." The plan was to give $330,888 to support 20 Chemung County organizations, and $63,392 to the Chemung County Red Cross.

Approximately 600 guests attended the dinner at the Armory in downtown Elmira. When it came time to introduce Reagan, the toastmaster, Elmira College President Dr. J. Ralph Murray, pointed out that Reagan was a graduate of Eureka College in Illinois and had been granted an honorary degree by that institution, "and so I would like to introduce to you Dr. Ronald Reagan, the Betty Furness of General Electric."

In the midst of the Cold War and in keeping with the philosophy he came to epitomize, Reagan addressed the crowd.

"The United Campaign is essential in the fight against communism, because wherever there is a symbol of democracy, communists are against it. Where democracy works, the communist has nothing to sell.

"Because of the list of industries right here in Elmira, this city ranks high on the communist infiltration list. While defending the ramparts of freedom from without, we must be careful the walls don't crumble by default from within. We are defending the last stronghold of freedom.

Let's not cast aside the garment we have worn for 200 years.

"We have been called materialists."

He then cited the heroism of American servicemen during war and the gifts to charities, asking if this represents materialism.

The newspaper reported that Reagan was "relaxed, spoke with conviction for a cause which he said has won full support of the film capital."

Unfortunately, the fund drive stalled at $449,000.

Ronald Reagan in the *Star-Gazette* Sept. 25. 1958 page 13

Notre Dame's auditorium.
Star-Gazette September 25, 1955 page 13

NOTRE DAME HIGH SCHOOL MARKS 65TH ANNIVERSARY
by James Hare

According to the *Star-Gazette* of September 25, 1955, young Tommy Nolan got set to take a photograph of Bishop James E. Kearney during the procession at the dedication of Notre Dame High School, but Tommy's flash camera failed. "The boy was downcast."

The bishop, learning about what happened, met Tommy after the exercises and "promised him an autographed portrait."

It appears that was the only glitch on Saturday, September 24, 1955, when Bishop Kearney, of the Roman Catholic Diocese of Rochester, blessed and dedicated the new school, "during impressive ceremonies which attracted nearly 1,000 Elmirans, clergymen and nuns from throughout the Rochester Diocese."

The program began at noon with the bishop leading a procession of altar boys, clergymen and an honor guard of the Fourth Degree Assembly of the Knights of Columbus. He blessed the building and foyer and offered a prayer: "… Fill them who teach here with the spirit of knowledge, wisdom and fear of the Lord. Support the pupils with heavenly assistance, so that they may grasp, retain and practice all useful and wholesome lessons, and in everything give honor to Thy name."

Elmira's Notre Dame High School was dedicated in 1955.

Mass was celebrated in the auditorium. Seated in the balcony were members of the Sisters of Mercy who staffed the school. The bishop thanked them for assuming the heavy debt to take over the school. It was noted that "the establishment in Elmira of the $1,600,000 new Notre Dame High School marks a major venture for the Sisters of Mercy who have served as educators in the Diocese of Rochester for almost a century."

A luncheon with over 300 people attending followed the Mass. Tours of the new building were provided.

According to W. Charles Barber, a local historian and newspaper editor, Catholic education in Elmira can be said to have two high water marks spaced some 70 years apart. The first was the institution of the parochial school at St. Peter & Paul soon after its dedication on July 19, 1857. The second was the establishment of the Elmira Catholic High School.

The high school opened in September of 1930 with 25 boys and girls taught by the Sisters of St. Joseph. They were temporarily located at St. Peter and Paul with the hope that the first year would bring about a demand for an individual building and a complete four-year course. In 1932, the school was relocated to the third floor (a climb of 52 steps) of St. Patrick's School. Because of increased enrollment, the Sisters of Mercy were asked to help form a staff. On June 26, 1934, nineteen students received their diplomas in St. Patrick's Church. They were the first graduating class of Elmira Catholic High School.

The year 1952 brought a dramatic development in Catholic school affairs. Bishop Kearney announced the purchase of a 25½-acre plot on lower Maple Avenue as the site for a large high school and accompanying facilities needed to operate it (14½ acres from Thomas P. McCann, and 11 acres from Raymond Guirey). The Sisters of Mercy would build and operate the school.

Located on the McCann parcel was a home built in 1791 and rebuilt in 1906. This would become the convent for the Sisters of Mercy. In 1963, it was announced that a $500,000 convent would be built to replace this house, which had been remodeled to accommodate the Sisters. The convent closed in 2014; it has been used for the school's international students for the last six years.

According to the Elmira *Advertiser* (August 29, 1953), construction of Notre Dame was part of a campaign by the Rochester Diocese to build four new high schools at a total cost of $5.5 million. Estimated cost for Notre Dame ranged from $1.4 million to $1.6 million. Catholics in Elmira pledged $616,010, more than $100,000 over the goal. The remainder was financed by the Sisters of Mercy. The Elmira architects selected were Haskell, Considine & Haskell. At the dedication, Bishop Kearney would thank Leo Considine, architect for the construction for his "personal consecration" to the school.

The Elmira *Advertiser* of February 12, 1953 reported that "a commemorative prayer with the words 'let the little children come to me' formally launched construction of the Notre Dame de Lourdes Catholic High School yesterday afternoon before an estimated gathering of more than 1,500 persons." The day celebrated "the Feast of Our Lady of Lourdes, who will be the patron of the school."

In January of 1955, Sister Mary Raphael, principal of the new high school, announced registration dates for February. Annual tuition was listed at $125 per student, payable in advance or on terms agreed to by school officials and parents. She also announced an innovation for Elmira schools, that all girls would be expected to wear a uniform, which would cost an estimated $14 and "using reasonable care, can go through her four years in high school with two outfits." Boys must wear neckties.

The school opened with 341 students. The faculty consisted of one priest, thirteen Sisters of Mercy, and two lay persons for grades 9-12.

Joe Manning, who had spent three years at Catholic High and would be a member of the first graduating class at Notre Dame (Class of '56), recalled that at the final assembly at the old school, the students "marched out with the Notre Dame fight song and not a dry eye." He also remembered that Notre Dame was a new experience with his class growing from 39 to 47.

His chemistry class, taught by Sister Carmela Coene, was the only one in the state to have 100% passing the New York State Regents. (When I asked him for a source, he said a "nun told me.") When he mentioned that to Sister Carmella on her 100th birthday in November 2008, she reminded him that his test was a close call.

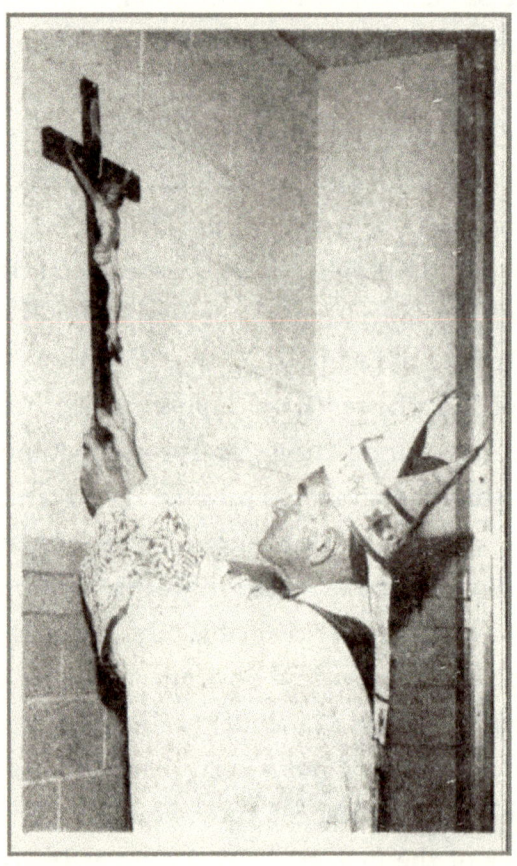

Bishop James E. Kearney affixed a crucifix to a wall at Notre Dame. *Star-Gazette* 25, 1955 page 3

ELMIRA COLLEGE'S 1919 COMMENCEMENT: FORMER PRESIDENT TAFT IN TOWN AMID LABOR TENSION
by James Hare

Wednesday, June 11, 1919, was a day of excitement in Elmira. Elmira College's 64th annual commencement exercises were held at the Park Church.

Fifty-eight young women received their degrees in a packed church sanctuary, and former U.S. President William Howard Taft delivered the commencement address.

An undertone of tension also pervaded the city as the major strike at the Willys-Morrow plant, which began on May 6, continued. On Wednesday evening, the Mozart Theater had been engaged by the Central Trades and Labor Assembly, with Frank D. Hawley, of the U.S. Department of Labor, speaking to employees and employers on the country's reconstruction problems. There was speculation that Taft might also speak at the Mozart that evening.

On Tuesday, May 6, the *Star-Gazette* had reported, "approximately 1,500 employees of the Willys-Morrow Company of this city walked out of the big plant where parts of the Willys-Overland automobiles are manufactured ... The employees ask for a 44-hour week. They are now working 48 hours before receiving overtime."

The paper noted that Willys plant President A.P. Morrow reacted strongly, citing "radical leaders in our factory" as the cause.

The Elmira strike was related to labor unrest at the Willys-Overland Company in Toledo, Ohio. Morrow called it a "failure." He called it "purely a sympathetic strike without any just cause or grievances or any consultation with the management."

John S. Hugg, of the Elmira Willys-Morrow shop committee, represented the employees. He claimed over 90% of the men were on strike. "Brothers, we are all out and out for a just cause," he was quoted. "We are going to remain out until this is settled. I implore you to maintain order. We will be better off as men and have nothing to be sorry for when it is all over."

At the time of the strike, 3,970 were employed at the plant.

Another concern at this time was reported in the May 10 *Star-Gazette*: "The Willys-Morrow strike hasn't a thing on Master Cupid's strike at the City Hall. Since May 5, City Registrar Sellen has issued no marriage licenses and since May 1 only four licenses have been procured. This is considered a very unusual condition and the officials who issue the licenses are unable to account for Cupid's inertia."

Meanwhile, as part of the EC graduation festivities, the commencement play, "Joan of Arc," was to be held. An ad in the June 4 *Star-Gazette* claimed it was "the most pretentious effort of the kind in the history of the college." It would be "correctly costumed and staged at unusual expense amid the gorgeous natural beauties of the campus amphitheater."

The production presented by the "100 Elmira College Girls" was scheduled for Friday and Saturday evenings, June 6 and 7. Unfortunately, because of rainy weather, the play was given in the Lyceum both nights. Because of improved weather, it was requested that the play be offered on Tuesday evening, June 10, on campus.

The Elmira College *Weekly* noted, "It was more beautiful than it was at the Lyceum on account of the natural setting. The coronation procession was also enlivened by the horses, which it was impossible to use in the Lyceum …"

Commencement exercises were held on Wednesday afternoon, June 11, to accommodate former President Taft's schedule. The Park Church

June 10, 1919. President Taft at Elmira College. *Star-Gazette*, page 14

had been selected as the site for the ceremonies to enable more people to hear Taft speak.

Upon arrival at about 1 p.m., Taft was greeted by attorney Hubert C. Mandeville, of the College board of trustees, and Sen. Seymour Lowman, chairman of the Chemung County Republican Committee. They had lunch at the City Club.

A strike leader at the Willys-Morrow plant, who was involved in planning the program at the Mozart, was asked if he intended to solicit Taft to act as an arbitrator in the strike. He responded, "No." But he did say, "If the opportunity is presented I shall tell him of the conditions here and if he should offer to act as an arbiter we would be glad to accept his services" (*Star-Gazette*, June 10, 1919).

When Taft was asked about speaking at the Mozart, he was unequivocal in his response. "I am not going to speak at any meeting on a labor issue … I know nothing of the merits of the situation here, but I shall take no part in the controversy" (*Star-Gazette*, June 11, 1919).

As scheduled, the graduation ceremonies took place at the Park Church. The College *Weekly* described the proceedings. With Merritt Welch, the church organist, playing the processional, "the members of the Class of 1919 marched to their seats through the Church Street door of the church, preceded by the members of the under classes and followed by members of the faculty and the board of trustees of the college. Bringing up the rear was William H. Taft, former president of the United States … Mr. Taft was cheered as his rotund personage came into view …"

The June 12 *Star-Gazette* called Taft's commencement address on the League of Nations "remarkable." Quoting Taft: "The League of Nations covenant does not create a super-sovereign … The League is a union of nations to suppress the spirits of conquest … to maintain and preserve the international commitment 'Thou shalt not steal.'"

After the conclusion of the festivities at the church, Taft was in the care of Dr. Frederick Lent, president of Elmira College, and Mrs. Lent. They would entertain him at their home. The day ended with the 25th commencement concert of the college music department for the 64th commencement.

Former President Taft spent the night in Elmira, leaving the next morning. The Willys-Morrow strike would last another eight months, ending in February of 1920.

FORMER PRESIDENT TAFT MAY SPEAK AT MOZART WEDNESDAY EVENING

Use of Mozart Theater Given To One of America's First Citizens by Committee in Charge of U. S. Labor Department Meeting — Final Answer Is Awaited From Mr. Taft—Hawley to Occupy Same Platform.

President Taft at the Mozart Theater. June 9, 1919, *Star-Gazette* page 7.

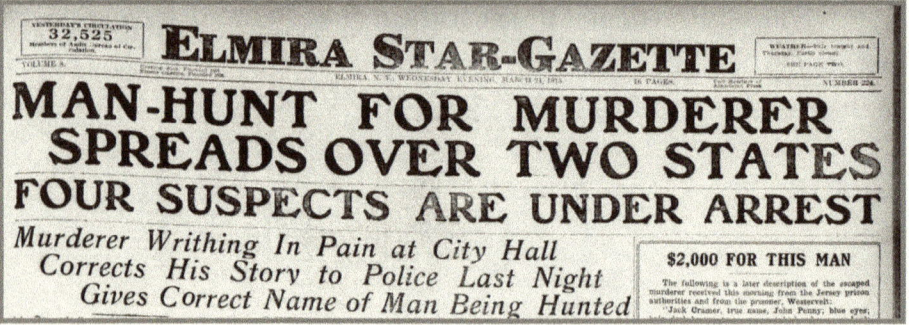

Star-Gazette headlines March 24, 1915 page 1

ELMIRA POLICE CHIEF AND DETECTIVE MURDERED
by James Hare

"Over all the countryside, the shimmering glow of automobile headlights betokened to anyone in hiding of the approach of a posse. Automobiles disregarded all speed limits as they sped over the pavements for the rural regions. Inside each car was a throng of man-hunters carrying shotguns, rifles, revolvers. All were armed to the teeth and prepared for any sort of an emergency." The March 24, 1915, *Star-Gazette* continued, "The experience of those who were members of searching parties after dark last night or even those who were entering barns, lumber yards, and freight cars yesterday afternoon was most thrilling. They did not know what moment the revolver carried by the outlaw might speak out its death-telling bark."

This automobile posse had been dispatched by Chemung County District Attorney Ely W. Personius and Captain Elvin D. Weaver of the Elmira Police Department at about 1 a.m. on March 24 in pursuit of the man suspected of the murder of Elmira Police Chief John J. Finnell the day before. Armed police officers, special deputies, soldiers of Company L, and citizens made up the posse. They were searching for Jack Penny, alias John (Jack) Cramer.

Penny and Edward Westervelt had come to Elmira on March 18. They were parolees from the New Jersey State Penitentiary, having served time for burglary. Upon arrival, they had booked a room at Mrs. Mary J. Collins' boarding house at 314 Baldwin Street. Soon after, reports of burglaries increased.

Elmira police Detective Sergeant Charles Gradwell was assigned to investigate. On March 23, Chief Finnell and Detective Gradwell, in response to leads, decided to call on Penny and Westervelt.

Erin Doane, Curator at the Chemung County Historical Museum, described what happened in an article on the September 2015 *Chemung Historical Journal*:

"Chief Finnell and Detective Gradwell arrived at the boarding house at about 3:30 in the afternoon. Mrs. Collins let the officers in then went to the backyard to hang some clothes. Both Westervelt and Penny were in the room this time. Gradwell told the men that he had brought the Chief, and they were going to talk a few minutes. He took off his overcoat and draped it over the chair. After a brief conversation, he told the men they had to go to headquarters to be searched. That was when the two suspects decided to flee.

"Westervelt dove toward the window, and Penny ran for the door. Chief Finnell grabbed Westervelt's leg and broke it as he dragged him from the window. Westervelt, in turn, pulled a revolver from his pocket and shot the Chief in the head at close range. He died almost immediately. Detective Gradwell pulled his gun from his pocket but was shot twice before he could return fire. The first bullet entered the left side of his body about four inches to the left of his spine, while the second entered his face at the left side of his jaw and went upward into his brain. Penny bolted the door, then he and Westervelt escaped out the window."

Westervelt and Penny were separated upon leaving the boarding house. Westervelt would be apprehended at the First Methodist Church just down the street later that day with a revolver having fired three shots. Penny escaped and became the subject of the aforementioned search by the posse.

The emotions surrounding this murder were volatile. In the *Star-Gazette* on December 2, 1978, Garth Wade wrote that upon Wester-

March 24, 1915 *Star-Gazette*, page 1. The address today is Elm Chevrolet's parking lot.

velt's arrest crowd's yelled, "lynch him...kill him." He also noted that when Captain Weaver (who would become the next Chief) found the bodies, "the sight almost drove the captain crazy with grief. He stiffened up, and the cold tears ran down his face." At the time of the Chief's funeral, the newspaper reported, "when grief steps in, all men think alike. Thousands of broken-hearted Elmirans filled the streets around the residence of the late police chief and the St. Patrick's church this morning. They didn't attend the funeral of the Chief of police, nor of a man who had laid his life down for the protection of others. They attended the funeral of "Hop" Finnell. They had lost a friend and were heartbroken. (*Star-Gazette*, March 27, 1915)

Westervelt would be tried in Binghamton and convicted of murder in the second degree. He was sentenced to twenty years to life at the Auburn prison. His defense for the Chief's murder was that Penny did it. He would serve fifteen years and be paroled in 1930 to Chemung County to face other indictments. A plea deal was arranged whereby Penny pleaded guilty to burglary, and the court dismissed the murder indictment on Finnell's death. He served five years of a seven-year sentence, being released in 1935. He died in New York City in 1952.

The search for Penny continued. On March 3, 1917, the *Star-Gazette* reported, "District Attorney Personius runs down Jack Penny serving with English Army in France only to find he is the wrong man." On June 2, 1920, the paper headlined "Police Now Feel Confident Fugitive Being Held In Oklahoma is Jack Penny; Elmira Officers Go To Identify Him." The officers planned to use the Bertillon system of measuring instruments to identify him (measure head and fingers, determine height and weight, record color of eyes). On June 11, it was reported that measurements and fingerprints "proved beyond a doubt" he was the wrong Penny.

On November 22, 1928, the *Star-Gazette* headline read "Elmirans Have Visions of Return of Murderer Penny When Arrest Reported."

However, the "swindler" captured in Los Angeles did not match the "Elmira" Penny. Garth Wade reported in his 1978 article that the "hunt turned up a man in Salt Run, Pennsylvania who matched Penny's description identically but wasn't Penny. Three men were detained in Hornell, and Mrs. Collins was taken to the Maple City to identify one of them as Penny. None was Penny. (*Star-Gazette*, December 3, 1978)

Elmira Police Chief Thomas J. Donnells doubted Penny's guilt. He told Garth Wade, "I have never found anything that has substantiated the claim that Penny was there. That was based on sort of a hearsay." As to why Westervelt escaped execution, according to Wade, Donnells believed that he was not executed because of the way he was treated after his arrest, held nearly twenty-four hours without medical treatment.

In January 2021, Elmira Police Chief Joseph Kane told me that the case is classified as "Office Review." In effect, there are no solvability factors present, and no further active investigative efforts will be made. The Chief also noted that four Elmira police officers have died in the line of duty. All the deaths took place on Baldwin Street.

March 11, 1915. *Star-Gazette* page 11.

OLD FOLKS ARE MADE HAPPIER

Members of Zonta Club Distribute Good Cheer and Christmas Gifts to Inmates at Home For the Aged.

December 22, 1919. *Star-Gazette*, page 15.

ZONTA CLUB
by James Hare

Chemung County District Attorney Raymond F. Nichols "has no use for the argument against the fair sex serving on juries" and said so when speaking to the Elmira Zonta Club on March 1. He told the club ladies, "There is only one reason, possibly two, why women would not make good jurors. The first criticism sometimes used is that women do not reason. They arrive at conclusions too quickly." The speaker stated that he did not believe this to be true. "The other argument is the matter of sympathy. Women with their motherly hearts are naturally more sympathetic than men." (*Star-Gazette* March 22, 1921).

It should be noted that Nichols was ahead of his time on the issue. Women did not begin serving on juries in New York State until September 5, 1937. (Civil Liberties History).

Almost a year earlier, the newspaper reported on May 25, 1920, that Attorney Richard Marlowe of the Chemung County Bar Association spoke about the Bar's campaign for Americanism and law and order. He "advised that the ladies of the club be living epistles of true Americanism giving the glad hand of welcome to the newcomer and making their problem lighter, that no seed of Bolshevism may find lodgement in their minds."

The president of Zonta, Mrs. Anna Presler, stated that, "the only way we could put the spirit of America into newcomers was for us to take them by the hand and share with them their problems and help them succeed in America as Americans." To that end, Zonta had hosted a party at the Neighborhood House in February for the "wives, sisters and mothers and not a few of the children of foreign-born Americans who have taken out papers since 1917...more than one hundred were in the party... and each guest was given a flag to take home." (*Star-Gazette*, February 27, 1920)

Another issue Zonta responded to was Near East Relief. William J. Howe of Binghamton spoke to the club as a representative of the Near East Relief Campaign. On January 13, 1920, the Elmira *Advertiser* reported his remarks: "The greatest thing in life is service and that these thousands and thousands of children (in Armenia and Syria) of the Near East will be what America makes them."

United States involvement in World War I brought many changes to the American social fabric. The war period brought an opportunity for women to demonstrate their ability in responsible executive positions. Women were being attracted to new fields of work. The idea of a classified club for professional and executive business women had an instant appeal. With the passage of the Equal Suffrage Law (19th Amendment) and impending ratification by the states, women were anxious to keep their new place in the world.

"So—a different type of club from any other existing women's club was formed. It was based on business representation as well as professionalism. Membership was made up of one woman from one type of business or profession—similar to the plan of Rotary and Kiwanis. (*Sunday Telegram* September 27, 1959)

Early in 1919, approximately one hundred women formed the Zonta Club in Buffalo. In September, a club was formed in Elmira. On November 8, 1919, in Buffalo, the Confederation of Zonta Clubs was created with the Elmira Zonta Club (eighteen charter members) as one of nine charter groups. "Zonta" is a Sioux Indian name meaning trustworthy and honest. In 1930 the organization became known as Zonta International.

The Elmira club's first president was Anna Presler. According to the May 1922 *Zontian* (the official publication of Zonta), she was "Pacifist. Prohibition Officer for four years - was preseptress at Cook Academy twelve years and was an auto enthusiast, until some reckless driver under an 'influence' smashed part of her car."

The commitment to service has been fundamental for Zonta. Women's issues, Near East Relief, and Americanization were early callings. They were also involved with "Thrift Campaigns" throughout Elmira to foster thrift and economy. Substantial support was provided to the Y.M.C.A. and the Y.W.C.A., and many activities with residents of the Home for the Aged were undertaken.

Socialization plays a significant role in the Zonta agenda. Weekly luncheons and monthly business meetings and programs have been part of their tradition. In 1968, the club acquired its own house. It was the former Mildred P. Fancher Nursing Home at 742 West First Street. Elmira, at that time, was the only club in the continental United States to own its own house. It serves as a location for a wide variety of activities and meetings.

Prominently displayed in Zonta House is a picture of fellow Zontian Amelia Earhart. She had become a member of the Boston Zonta Club in 1928. On Friday, November 13, 1936, less than eight months before her disappearance, she spoke at the First Baptist Church in Elmira about "Adventures in the Air." The Zonta Club was one of the sponsors of her appearance. The *Star-Gazette* noted that she "looks nearer pre-voting age than her 38 years…She came by automobile because of the expense involved of hopping her ten-passenger short distances. Besides, she doesn't like to leave her car out of the garage at night, 'so what do you think I could do with my pet airplane if I could not find a hangar." She stayed at the Mark Twain Hotel for the night.

On October 5 of this year (2019), a torch will arrive to be permanently housed in Elmira. District Two of Zonta International is circulating the torch to celebrate one hundred years since its founding. In the words of Zonta's code, "To honor my work and to consider it a service opportunity."

From the October 1920 *Zontian* (to the tune of "Mickey")

> *Zonta, Jolly Zonta*
> *We're the only club in view*
> *With our Janes and Ann Elizas,*
> *Pretty Polly and Susie*
> *Mary Melinda, too—*
> *Line up for a size up*
> *Show the old Town what we'll do,*
> *For tis a live bunch*
> *And a tried bunch*
> *And we're out for ELMIRA*
> *Pledged to ELMIRA true.*

'NEGLECTED' PIONEER CRYSTAL EASTMAN WENT FROM ELMIRA TO THE NATIONAL WOMEN'S HALL OF FAME

by James Hare

On March 24, 1911, the day before the Triangle Shirtwaist Company fire in New York City — which left 147 dead — the New York Court of Appeals had declared the state's compulsory worker's compensation law unconstitutional. Largely because of the fire, that law was back in force in 1913.

Elmira's own Crystal Eastman had drafted that worker's compensation law.

According to the National Women's Hall of Fame, "Eastman was one of only a few hundred women lawyers in the early twentieth century. Her pioneering report, *Work Accidents and the Law* (published in book form in 1910), led New York Gov. Charles Evans Hughes to appoint her the first woman on

Crystal Eastman.
Image courtesy of Wikipedia

New State's Commission on Employer's liability and Causes of Industrial

Accidents, Unemployment and Lack of Farm Labor in 1909. As a member of that commission, Eastman drafted the country's first workers' compensation law. That legislation became the model for workers' compensation throughout the nation. Then, during Woodrow Wilson's administration, Eastman became investigating attorney for the United States Commission on Industrial Relations."

Crystal Eastman was a human-rights activist and suffragist who co-authored the first Equal Rights Amendment and helped found the ACLU. Crystal believed workers' compensation was essential for preventing accidents because it "makes every serious accident a considerable cost to an employer and thus insures his invaluable cooperation ... in promoting safety" (from *The Three Essentials for Accident Prevention* by Crystal Eastman).

Crystal Catherine Eastman (June 25, 1881 to July 8, 1928) arrived in Elmira at age 13 in 1894. She was the third of four children. Her parents, the Revs. Samuel and Annis Ford Eastman, had been appointed assistants to the Rev. Thomas K. Beecher at the Park Church, succeeding him upon his passing in 1900.

Annis Ford Eastman was one of the first women to be ordained in the Congregational Church. Shortly before her death in 1910, she would write the eulogy for Mark Twain, who had died earlier that same year. Samuel Eastman would serve Park Church until 1917.

Crystal attended school in Elmira, graduating from Elmira Free Academy in 1899. After high school, Crystal attended Vassar College graduating in 1903. She received an M.A. in sociology from Columbia University in 1904. In 1907, she was second in the class at New York University Law School. She was admitted to the bar at age 26.

Crystal would marry twice, the first time to Wallace J. Benedict in 1911. They divorced in 1916 after his infidelity. "She refused alimony, telling newspapers across the country that 'marriage is a link, not a handcuff' and 'no self-respecting feminist would accept alimony — it is a relic and would be her admission that she can't take care of herself" ("Crystal Eastman, A Revolutionary Life," digital recovery project).

Her second marriage (1916) to British editor and antiwar activist Walter Fuller resulted in two children and an unconventional lifestyle. She published an article, "Marriage Under Two Roofs," in 1923, explaining the success of a married couple with children living apart. "By offering greater autonomy for women," she proclaimed, "it created stronger, happier families as well as a more authentic experience of sexual desire and marital love."

On October. 7, 2000, Crystal Eastman was inducted into the National Women's Hall of Fame.

The New World Encyclopedia notes, "Crystal Eastman has been called one of the United States' most neglected leaders … she disappeared from history for fifty years."

Discussion of the Equal Rights Amendment in the 1970s and '80s stimulated another look. Local activists in the Chemung County Council of Women led the effort to recognize her. Cindy Emmer, a local activist and member of the Professional Employees Federation, first reawakened interest in Crystal in a presentation at a union-sponsored women's program. Faith Hallock, who attended that meeting, took the ball and led the charge to have her admitted. In fact, Crystal's granddaughter acknowledged Faith at the induction ceremony.

The Hall of Fame website notes that in addition to workers' compensation, "Eastman also struggled to further women's rights — first suffrage and later equal rights — as co-author of the first Equal Rights Amendment. During World War I, she was a leader of the peace movement, working with Carrie Chapman Catt to organize the Carnegie Hall meeting that led to the founding of the Women's Peace Party of New York — later renamed the Women's International League of Peace and Freedom … Eastman became Executive Secretary of the Women's Peace Party.   A leading advocate of civil liberties and the rights of conscientious objectors during World War I, she joined Norman Thomas and Roger Baldwin in founding the American Civil Liberties Union as the 'watch dog' organization protecting Americans' rights under the Bill of Rights and providing legal assistance to those whose rights may have been violated, regardless of partisan persuasion."

In the book she edited, *Crystal Eastman on Women and Revolution*, she noted, "her life by its very example embodied a threat to customary order. 'Freedom is a large word,' she wrote in 1920. It demanded a large struggle, a long battle. She was committed to that struggle, and the range and intensity of her energy and spirit served her well."

Freda Kirchway, a contemporary of Crystal Eastman, wrote, "When she spoke to people— whether it was to a small committee or a swarming crowd — hearts beat faster ... she was for thousands a symbol of what the free woman might be."

ROSS GILMORE MARVIN
by James Hare

Marvin Park is located at the intersection of Lake Street and Union Place. It is dedicated to the memory of Ross Gilmore Marvin, "Elmira's intrepid adventurer, whose desires to penetrate the great unknown region of the North was unconquerable, irrepressible." (*Star-Gazette*, April 5, 1931) Originally a huge boulder located on the site marked his memory. In 1989, at the request of a Marvin descendant the boulder was relocated to the southeast corner of Lake and Church Streets with the hope that it might be more visible.

The *Star-Gazette* noted on December 3, 1989 that, "For the uninformed, Elmira-born, Cornell University educated Marvin was a scientist who served as first assistant to Admiral Robert E. Peary on the latter's pioneering expeditions to the North Pole. Marvin

Ross Gilmore Marvin.
Image courtesy of Wikipedia

died at age 29, on one such expedition in April 1909 succumbing to either the thin ice and Arctic waters or to a rifle bullet fired by a slighted Eskimo, depending on the account." **A question to ponder is did Marvin accidentally fall through the ice into the Arctic Ocean, or did he go mad and provoke an Eskimo into shooting him?**

Another interesting question is who actually discovered the North Pole? On September 7, 1909, The New York *Times* headline read, "Peary Discovers the North Pole After Eight Trials in 23 Years." A week earlier, the headline of The New York *Herald* read, "The North Pole is Discovered by Dr. Frederick A Cook." Cook claimed to have reached the pole on April 21, 1908. According to the *Smithsonian Magazine*, in 1988, the National Geographic Society, a major sponsor of Peary's expedition concluded his evidence never proved his claim, and that Cook's claim had been neither proved or disproved. In 1909 journalist Lincoln Steffens hailed the battle over Peary's and Cook's competing claims as the story of the century. "Whatever the truth is, the situation is as wonderful as the Pole. And whatever they found there, those explorers, they have left there a story as great as a continent."

Ross Marvin was born in Elmira on January 28, 1880 to Mr. and Mrs. Edward Marvin. He lived at 409 Dewitt Avenue. His father died when he was five. He attended Public School No. 1 (Beecher) graduating with honors. From there he went to Elmira Free Academy graduating in 1899. He enjoyed athletics and won a scholarship to Cornell University. He worked his way through school and also attended the New York Nautical School. The *Sunday Telegram* of April 8, 1979 noted that, "his life of science began immediately after commencement when he was recommended to Peary in 1905 by a friend and former colleague Louis Bement who was a merchant in Ithaca. Bement, was familiar with students at Cornell. He told Peary, "I have a young man by the name of Marvin, and he is a marvel." (*Telegram*, September 12, 1909) Ross made his first trip to the Arctic that year. Four years later he made his second and last."

On his first expedition with Peary, Marvin went as a chief scientist. When that proved unsuccessful, he became a professor at Mercersburg (Pennyslvania) Academy for a brief time, then returned to Cornell as an instructor in astronomy and other sciences. In July 1908, he again joined Peary for an Arctic expedition. It consisted of "seven explorers, 17 picked Eskimos, 133 of the best dogs in Greenland and 19 sledges." They set sail on the SS *Roosevelt*, Peary's Arctic ship. (*Sunday Telegram* April 8, 1979)

Marvin kept a diary during his journey. His last entry was December 8, 1908, "The holidays are coming soon and, of course, my thoughts will be of home and my family. I should prefer to spend them with them if it were possible, but if all goes well, I will count myself lucky to be back in civilization a year hence."

The newspaper goes on to report that Marvin was the leader of a support party whose job was to forge ahead and establish advance camps for Peary's group which would make the final push through "ice barriers, terrific winds, 59 below-zero temperatures and the 133 mile final lap."

Marvin's support party returned to the ship. In a three page message found in a seal skin bag attached to his sledge, dated March 25, 1909 he wrote, "This is to certify that I turn back from this point with the third supporting party. Commander Peary advancing with nine men in the party...." That is believed to be his last recorded writing.

On April 10, 1909, Marvin died without ever reaching the North Pole. News did not reach Elmira until September 8, 1909. Commander Peary sent a telegram to Louis Bement in Ithaca which read, "Break the news of Marvin's death to his mother immediately before she sees it in the paper. Drowned April 10, 1909 - 45 mile north of Cape Columbia while returning from 86 degrees 38 minutes North Latitude. Great loss to me

"Battle Harbor, Via Cape Race, N. F.,
"6:45 P. M., Sept. 8, 1909.
"L. C. Bement, Ithaca, N. Y.:
"Break news of Marvin's death to his mother immediately, before she sees it in the papers. Drowned April 10 forty-five miles north of Cape Columbia while returning from 86 degrees 38 minutes north latitude. Great loss to me and to expedition. Every member sends deepest sympathy.
"PEARY."

Image from the *Star-Gazette*, Sept. 9, 1909, page 1

and to expedition. Every member sends deepest sympathy—Peary." The headline the next day in the *Star-Gazette* was in red ink. The story was, he had fallen through the ice. (File from Chemung County Historical Society)

But now, the rest of the story. In 1926, seventeen years after Marvin's reported death by drowning one of his Inuit (Eskimo) companions confessed to shooting him. Cousins Inuksutoq and Kudlooktoo who had been with Marvin, had become Christian and were moved at a prayer meeting where Kudlooktoo stated "Ross Marvin did not die because he drowned, but because I shot him."

In an article from *Crime Scribe*, Robert Walsh wrote that, "according to the two Inuits, Marvin's personality had become progressively more irrational and disturbed as the expedition wore on." It appeared that Marvin was planning to leave Inuksutoq out on the tundra which would have meant certain death. Marvin also refused to let Kudlooktoo share his igloo.

The men were questioned by a Danish explorer admitting that to protect themselves Marvin was killed. According to Walsh, "what actually happened is unclear…either the truth (or a well-concocted lie)"

In 1954, Peary's daughter, who knew Kudlooktoo, stated that she believed the original story of Marvin's death. She felt the Eskimo's confession was "induced by religious hysteria and an attempt to please the white man by a having a sin to confess." (Historical Society file)

The Rev. John Bedzyk stands before his first church, founded in an old shirt factory on East Henry Street in 1944.

Star-Gazette image August 26, 2001, page 24

PENTECOSTAL TABERNACLE
by James Hare

"In 1934, John remembers hearing about a Wesleyan Camp meeting in Chambers, New York. At twelve years of age, he and a large group of Ukrainian children piled into and onto a 1926 Essex. John rode straddling a headlight. They were hungry for God. Every one of this group of young people was saved that day." (*Herald-Examiner* April 1991)

John Bedzyk was the son of Michael and Anna Bedzyk. Michael, a Ukrainian immigrant, had come from Zahutyn province in Poland around 1910 at age 16. In 1914 he took a job at the former Eclipse Machine Company in Elmira Heights, where he met and married Anna Moskal. They settled in the Ukrainian community. John was born in 1922. Bedzyk described his parents for John Cleary's Neighbors column in the *Star-Gazette* in 2001, "They were godly parents, but they weren't always that way. My father was a gambler and a drinker and a wife-beater. But God changed his life. My mother prayed, and God showed her there would be a church in Elmira, and her son was going to be the pastor of that church."

When the Great Depression hit in 1929 and work became scarce, the Bedzyks moved to a farm in Sullivanville. "John attended a one-room school in Sullivanville and 'skipped' second and seventh grades. It seems that he was the only one in second grade, so his teacher moved him up a grade. The same thing happened in seventh grade." (*Telegram* September 1, 1974). In 1936 the family was foreclosed on and moved back to the Heights.

John graduated from Edison High School at age 16, eighth in his class.

After graduation in 1938, John entered the Zion Bible Institute in East Providence, Rhode Island, at a tuition cost of $10 a year. When he graduated in 1941, he became the assistant pastor of a Pentecostal Church in West Virginia. Within two weeks, he was home with tuberculosis. He spent time in the Chemung County Sanatorium or at Biggs Memorial Hospital in Ithaca for the next three years.

The seeds of a "new beginning" were sown in 1943 when his family purchased a tent and held revival meetings on Maple Avenue. When released from the hospital in the fall of that year, "Brother" John began walking the streets of Elmira's Southside, looking for a place to found his church. (*Telegram* September 1, 1974) While strolling by the intersection of Pennsylvania Avenue and Henry Street (site of Tops Plaza) in the summer of 1944, he came upon the old Springstead Shirt Factory, which had been empty for years. For $20 per month, it would become the home of the Pentecostal Tabernacle.

Katherine Mattoon, a long time member of the church and the former principal of the Elmira Christian Academy, wrote in her history of the church, *Elmira Christian Center Pentecostal Tabernacle Its History 1944-2009*, "With a small expenditure of money and many long hours of work, the old shirt factory became a church. Both the money and the hard work came from the Bedzyk family. On Friday, August 18, 1944, twenty-five people attended the first service of the Pentecostal Tabernacle. People from Brother Love's church in Corning came. The offering was $6.50." Brother John described that first service, "my father was the usher, my mother led the prayer, my brother led the song service, my sister played the piano, and I preached."(*Telegram* September 1, 1974)

Katherine Mattoon noted that "the church seated 125 with camp meeting benches. Babies who fell asleep would occasionally roll off the benches onto the floor. Theater seats replaced the benches in 1946. People pledged and paid for the seats at 60 cents each...."

From its' opening in 1944, the Pentecostal Tabernacle was an energetic congregation. A series of tent meetings were held beginning in 1947. In 1950 a Tent Cathedral was established at East Miller and Falck Streets for the Vineyard Healing Campaign. Mattoon wrote that "establishing a bus ministry was a pioneering effort…our first bus route was to Pine City in 1947. The bus was a 1925 Indiana bought from a junkyard for $75." At its high point, there would be twenty-two routes.

By 1950, it was time for a new church. To raise funds, "Sacrifice Sundays" were held where all money received was set aside for construction. In addition, Brother John's father mortgaged his property to raise funds. Construction began at 235 East Miller Street in August 1950, with the congregation moving in February 1951. While the building was only a "shell" at that point, Brother John noted that the church membership pitched in to complete the interior. "They saved us thousands of dollars…without the volunteers, we could never have done it." (*Telegram* September 1, 1974)

The Pentecostal Tabernacle became the Elmira Christian Center.

In 1969, the Elmira Christian Academy was founded.

According to Garth Wade (*Telegram* November 11, 1973), "Mr. Bedzyk began his school, kindergarten through sixth grade. He's added a grade a year since reaching 10th grade this year. The church borrowed $200,000 last year to build a three-story school located behind the church…it costs $50 a month, ten months a year, to send a child to the school." Brother John said the school began as a "divine urge" 20 years ago.

The 47-year history of the Elmira Christian Academy came to an end with the Class of 2016. At its height, 220 students have enrolled in kindergarten through 12th grade.

The founding of the Pentecostal Tabernacle and the growth of the Elmira Christian Center has been a Bedzyk family calling. Brother John's parents and siblings were there at the beginning. In 1952, Sister Roberta joined when Bedzyk married Roberta Jean White from Clarks Summit, Pennsylvania.

Katherine Mattoon has written that, "from the beginning, she was willing to do whatever was needed: knock on doors and invite people to church, teach, preach, show hospitality, clean, sing, drive bus, but most of all pray." They had two children, Bonnie and Paul.

Brother John passed away at age 82 in 2004. His grandsons have accepted the call. The Reverend Matthew Bedzyk is the Senior Pastor and is ably assisted by his brother Associate Pastor The Reverend Mitchell Bedzyk.

On February 23, 2021, the church voted to change its' name from the Elmira Christian Center to Emmanuel Community Church. This was done according to the post on their website for two reasons. "First, it was to celebrate the completion of our seven-year revitalization effort...the second reason for our name change was to help clarify our identity as a church." The new name allows for keeping the acronym ECC and according to the post, "this would not only avoid much confusion among our own congregation and others in the community, but also honor our church's past and God's faithfulness to us over the years, as well as indicate a new chapter in our church's history."

* Disclaimer from both authors: That while we cannot change the past, we can acknowledge it, learn from it and move forward together. This story includes negative depictions and/or mistreatment of people or cultures. These stereotypes were wrong then and are wrong now. Rather than remove this content, we want to acknowledge its harmful impact, learn from it and spark conversation to create a more inclusive future together.

MINSTRELSY
by James Hare

"Tonight at the Lyceum, Quinlan & Wall finish their first season on the road with their own minstrel company, the most successful first season that has ever been recorded in the annals of minstrelsy. From one end of the country to the other, the performance promoted by 'Dan' Quinlan and 'Jimmy' Wall has been pronounced the most artistic ever attempted in this popular class of entertainment. Elmirans feel a certain degree of pride in this achievement as the founder and senior partner of this celebrated minstrel firm is a native of Elmira and one of the most popular of Elmira's citizens." (*Star-Gazette*, May 7, 1903)

On July 28, 1898, The Elmira *Daily Gazette and Free Press*, promoting the "biggest opening night in the history of the city," described the forthcoming "beautiful street parade" with "George Wilson, the greatest of all minstrels will march before his model minstrels." The paper observed that "minstrelsy is the distinctly American form of amusement and is the original contribution of this country to the gayety of nations, and it is a splendid offering."

In a review of the Cohan-Harris Minstrel show at the Lyceum on June 20, 1910, the *Star-Gazette* noted that "Elmira has seen minstrelsy exemplified since antebellum days."

Edwin S. Grosvenor wrote in the Winter 2019 edition of *American Heritage* that the "furor over the use of blackface by Virginia's governor and attorney general, while they were in college, reminds us of a sad chapter in our history—the long tradition of minstrel shows in which whites covered their faces with burnt cork or greasepaint." The topic is in the news again as companies review branding that stems from minstrelsy for product lines such as Aunt Jemima and Uncle Ben's. The College of William and Mary professor Chinua Thelwell, who has explored the history of minstrelsy states that, "racist minstrel shows are part of America's cultural legacy. We Americans need to acknowledge this history…" While minstrelsy is widely considered unacceptable in mainstream culture—that was not always the case. The story of Elmira reflects that.

I must admit that I was taken aback to learn that my church, the former Centenary Methodist Episcopal Church, was one of many churches which produced minstrel shows in the late 1920s and early 1930s. The shows were performed by the Senate Baraca Class of the Sunday School and performed in the church gym. According to *The History of Park Church*, The Men's Own group, which was created in 1913, sponsored a minstrel show for a great many years. It "was a pleasant feature of the church's social life as well as a source of revenue." Newspapers reflect the scope of minstrelsy in the city. In May 1912, the Masonic Glee Club sponsored a minstrel show at Rorick's Glen. The Elmira College Class of 1913 presented a minstrel show in the college chapel. February 17, 1936, *Star-Gazette* headlined "Public Invited To Reformatory Minstrel Show." The musical and drama production had "a cast of 100."

Quinlan and Wall Imperial Minstrels was an Elmira-based operation. Dan Quinlan (1863-1940) was born here. He worked at the Rolling Mills and lived and worked in Danbury, Connecticut, before returning. In 1883 he hooked up with a minstrel show rehearsing in Elmira. According to the book "Monarch's of Minstrelsy" he became a property man and then "rose successfully to the positions of stage manager, interlocutor, manager and finally proprietor.

His obituary noted that, "for many years Quinlan's name was in the lights and on the billboards from one end of the country to the other." (*Star-Gazette* July 13, 1940)

James (Jimmy) Wall (1863-1927) was associated with Quinlan in the ownership of the Imperial Minstrels. "Jimmy" Wall was a "black face comedian" who was described as the "international champion of the merry sons of laughter." (*Star-Gazette* September 10, 1903)

Two other Elmirans of minstrel fame were John J. Finnell and Charles S. Blaisdell. On May 20, 1904 the Elmira *Evening Star* reported that "Hop" and "Bill" were the "Funniest Pair of Entertainers That Ever Came Down the Elmira Pike." Finnell was given much credit for the creation and success of the Father Mathews Minstrels sponsored by the Father Mathews Society. The paper noted that "Big Bill Blaisdell was in terms of minstrelsy the 'whole show' in himself…he is a valuable addition to Elmira's entertainers."

An undated article found in the archives at the Chemung County Historical Society describes another aspect of minstrelsy. Robert Mack was a caretaker at the Chemung Canal Trust Company who had "a complete surprise…when a friend left a roll of about $200 in green money at the bank as a gift for the faithful doorkeeper." Upon examination, he found the bills, each of the $10 denominations, were phony. They were stage money used in theatrical work and for advertising. "Among the specimens is the stage money bearing the advertisement of the 'Callender Colored Minstrels', which first appeared in Elmira in 1872. The show appeared annually at the first Elmira Opera House." Robert Mack was African American, and his parents "were leading company members many years and accompanied the troupe on two trips over the British Isles. On the second trip abroad, little Bob accompanied them." Bob Mack Sr. "was a comedian of much ability; he rode a horse at the head of the minstrel company's parade…he sounded the bugle calls between selections by the band in the parade." He died in 1885. His widow and son lived at 664 Dickinson Street.

Author and historian Marc Aronson has observed that Duke Ellington, Frederick Douglas, and W. E. B. Dubois "wanted to scrub off the burnt cork and show African Americans as individuals, not clownish distortions. This critique of minstrelsy continues to shape conversation today. But it is also important to understand what the strange yearning seen in minstrelsy reveals---both yesterday and today. Minstrelsy allowed black and white society to touch while maintaining distance." (July 22, 2018, *Washington Post*)

Minstrelsy is an uncomfortable part of Elmira's history. In telling the story, one does not want to mollify the resistance to the underlying racism of "white faces corked in black." We should understand that it served to reinforce the critical aspects of racism. To remember, one hopes will help us to "overcome."

Dan Quinlan, photo courtesy of author.

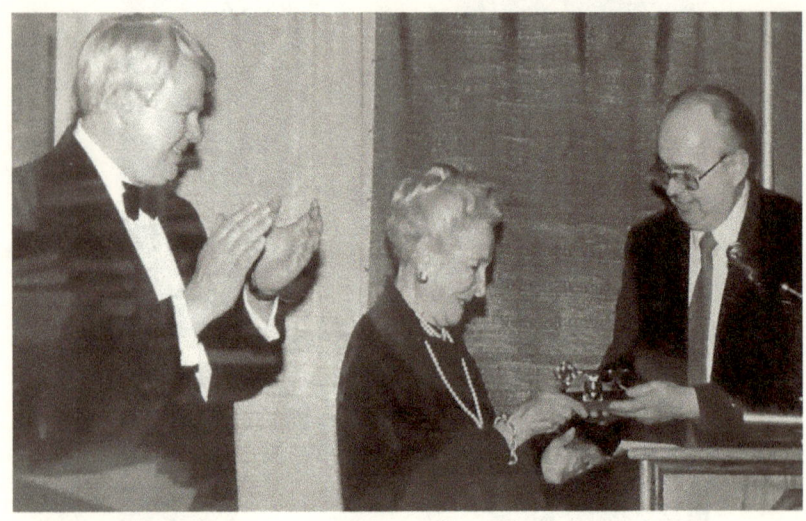

Former Elmira College President, Thomas Meier, Helen Hayes, and James Hare, Photo courtesy of the author.

ELMIRA COLLEGE "FIRST LADIES"
by James Hare

In March of 1991, as mayor of Elmira, I had the honor to present the Key to the City to Miss Helen Hayes, "The First Lady of the American Theater." It was a special thrill for me as we both shared the experience of performing in the play "Harvey."

She portrayed Vita Louise and I Vita's brother Elwood P. Dowd.

Of course, when she did the play on Broadway, Jimmy Stewart played Elwood. I played the Clemens Center.

Helen Hayes was in Elmira to attend the premiere of the Elmira College production of "Crimes in the Old Brewery" by Tim Kelly, the winner of the College's third Play Writing Contest. Miss Hayes was a special guest because she was an honorary alumna of the college. She had received a Doctor of Letters degree in 1937, noting that "nothing has touched my heart as much as that first degree." (*Star-Gazette*, March 8, 1991)

The June 15, 1937, Vermont Burlington *Free Press* reported: "Helen Hayes, actress, became Helen Hayes doctor of letters here today and confessed herself 'terribly frightened but awfully humbled by the experience. She blushed self-consciously as President William S. A. Pott read the sonorous claim on which Elmira College awarded the honorary degree:

> *By your activity and your devotion to the highest standards of your profession, you have ennobled and enriched the American stage and screen and at the same time furnished the young womanhood of America a conspicuous example of how a great career may be combined with the greatest of all professions—that of home-making.*

Miss Hayes said afterward that it was worse than a first night. But I wish I could have every one of those beautiful words tattooed on me...."

In her letter of acceptance to Dr. Pott, Hayes wrote, "I shall come to Elmira on June 14 to receive the degree in person. Nothing would keep me away. Will you be so kind as to let me know well in advance just what I am to do during my visit to the College? And may I offer up a prayer that no speeches are required."

On June 9, 1930, the *Star-Gazette* reported that, "The first institution to grant degrees to women conferred the honorary degree of Doctor of Laws today on the First Lady of the Land. Mrs. Lou Henry Hoover, the wife of President Herbert Hoover, was granted the honorary degree by the trustees of Elmira College at their annual session this morning."

The newspaper reported two days later that "unfortunately Mrs. Hoover, owing to a recent injury, could not come to Elmira to personally receive the degree. Mrs. Jennie C. Fassett would act as a proxy for Mrs. Hoover when the degree was conferred and would personally convey the parchment to Mrs. Hoover in Washington, a mission which she accepted with her accustomed grace." The paper noted that "Mrs. Hoover…has been actively interested in work among young women, a work which has been rewarded with excellent results. Long has she been a counselor and guiding spirit in the Girl Scout movement, and at every available opportunity, she has aided in the advancement of young womanhood."

On May 11, 1932, Mrs. Hoover was finally able to visit Elmira. The *Star-Gazette* reported that a "big crowd stands in the drizzling rain to greet First Lady." Upon arrival, Mrs. Hoover said, "I am glad that I belong to Elmira." She was welcomed by Dr. Frederick Lent, President of Elmira College, and Miss Emily Hull, President of the Student Government Association. A tour of the campus included visiting some classes, followed by a "chapel" at 11:00.

Various presentations were made, according to the Elmira College *Weekly* of May 11. The publication also reported that Mrs. Hoover "advised students to leave Elmira not to get so attached to the little things that they will not find time for the bigger things." A reception at Cowles Hall was next, with lunch at 2:30.

Mrs. Hoover, with Dr. Lent, planted a "new elm sprig" next to the pond on campus below Cowles Hall. Miss Jane More, a local girl scout, presented a bouquet of roses to the First Lady.

Following her visit, Mrs. Hoover wrote to Dr. Lent, "I can feel now that I am really a member of the Elmira alumnae, having taken part in its life, even though for so short a time."

The story of Mrs. Benjamin Harrison, Elmira '79, widow of the President of the United States, Benjamin Harrison, is very interesting. Of our three ladies, she is the only one who actually attended Elmira College. She was a student in the English Preparatory program from 1875-76. She is considered a member of the Class of 1879.

Mary Lord Harrison lived a long life, 1858-1948. She was the widowed niece of Benjamin Harrison's wife, Caroline. Mary's first husband, Walter Dimmick, had died in 1882. She lived in the White House for two years when her aunt Caroline died of tuberculosis in 1892.

Four years after Caroline died, in 1896, the former President married Mary Lord Dimmick. He was in his middle sixties, and she was in her late thirties. According to the Presidential History Blog: "Mary Dimmick and Benjamin Harrison had no blood between them, but they had grown close during those White House years…

Russell and Mamie, Harrison's children, and Mary Dimmick's blood first cousins were scandalized…They declined to attend the wedding…a year later, when Harrison and his new bride had a baby, the estrangement …was complete and permanent…Russell and Mamie never spoke to their father again." When Harrison died in 1901, his children did not attend the funeral.

After the death of the former President, Mary "kept to the end a surprising physical vigor and an unfading interest in politics…she attended Republican conventions and took part in the campaigns." (unidentified newspaper article) She was also active in Elmira College alumnae activities, honorary chair of an alumnae fundraising effort with Helen Hayes, and appearing at events with Lou Hoover.

In the Elmira College archive files is a handwritten but unidentified letter with a description of "Mary Lord Harrison."

It notes, "when we think of her, we still smile, as she always smiled at us. She was so friendly-so interesting, so gay. It was not her manner - it was herself."

FRANK E. BUNDY
by James Hare

During the annual Ghost Walk at Woodlawn Cemetery, sponsored by the Chemung County Historical Society in 2019, the grave site of Frank E. Bundy was a stop. His ghost spoke to the visitors, "It's been 84 years since my death, and I still have a bad reputation in this city. It's not fair…at the tail end of the 19th century, I was a rising star. My father was a grocer, but I had ambition. I was going places. I was a businessman, entrepreneur, politician, and popular man-about-town. The 1890s were my decade. Then it all came crashing down around me, and it's just not fair."

The Elmira *Daily Gazette* of February 5, 1900, reported:

"The Democratic city convention held at the city hall Saturday evening was one of the most enthusiastic and harmonious ever held in this city…The mention of the name of City Chamberlain (Treasurer) Frank E. Bundy as the nominee for mayor of our beautiful city was greeted with tremendous applause…in fact, it looked for a time as if the delegates and their friends would never get through cheering. Mr. Bundy's nomination was unanimous. He is a young man of the most sterling business principles."

A little over a month later, on March 28, the paper noted, "Mr. Bundy presents the appearance of a man who has just risen from an attack of the most severe fever of many months duration. He is a wrecked man… As Mr. Bundy walked to his seat on the prisoner's bench, several people remarked that he looked like a condemned man walking to the death chair."

WHAT HAPPENED?

His ghost was not sure when the trouble started. He had not wanted to join the family business. "I dabbled in several business ventures: manufacturing, real estate, insurance, publishing, even groceries. The problem is, to start your own business, you need some start-up capital. To get that, you need rich friends." Frank became a man-about-town. He was selected Eminent Commander of the Elmira Encampment No 51 Knights of St. John and Malta, President of the Kanaweola Cycle Club, and active in various other organizations. In 1898 the Frank E. Bundy Manufacturing Company was formed with Bundy as Treasurer. The *Daily Gazette* on October 27 reported the company would be conducted on a large scale. It "made acetylene gas lamps of all kinds such as bicycle lamps, carriage and hack lamps, table lamps, street lamps, physician lamps, fire department lamps, and engineers torches." Bundy entertained on a high scale and maintained a high cost of living.

At age 31, he was appointed Assistant City Chamberlain for 1892 and 93. He became City Chamberlain in 1894, serving until 1900. He soon began reaping the benefits. His ghost explains it best. "I swear I never set out to embezzle. I couldn't help it. It was just too easy.

"Here's how I did it. People would pay their property taxes, and I would mark all the payments down in my personal ledger noting which payments I'd taken for myself - generally, the ones who had paid in cash. In another ledger, the official ledger, I would put only some of them down as being paid and write off my take as unpaid taxes. Sometimes to make up the difference, I'd issue a second tax bill to the city's biggest companies, and they'd just pay it as a matter of course. Every year, the city's wealthiest set would put up bonds to help cover any tax shortfalls, so no one ever really felt the impact.

The Bundy Lamp

And then it all went wrong. Fred Fox, treasurer from the Lackawanna Railroad, noticed that his company was being double billed for taxes. He brought it to the City Council, and the jig was up." The Council began an investigation that very afternoon. *"I confessed to my friend and lawyer, former mayor Fred Collin, I'd embezzled $84,495 in city funds. That's about $2.5 million today."*

The April 17 *Daily Gazette* reported that after confessing his guilt to his attorney, Bundy "went home, and it was reported that he is under the care of Dr. Theron A. Wales, who was compelled to administer morphine to his patient."

Bundy would be indicted on two counts, "grand larceny in the first degree" and "misappropriation of city funds and the falsification of accounts." (*Daily Gazette*, April 26)

Bundy was convicted and sentenced to six and one-half years in the Auburn prison. According to newspaper reports, "a determined effort was made by friends of Bundy to get him placed in an easy position in prison.

Nearly every man in the force of prison employers who ever lived in Elmira has been approached by people from that city on behalf of Bundy. For several days past, Elmirans have been in the city using their influence to get Bundy in a soft place." He was assigned to the shop. (Undated Auburn *Advertiser*)

After serving his sentence in Auburn, Bundy relocated to New York City. He reappeared in the newspaper (*Star-Gazette*, December 27, 1906) when it was reported that Bundy "requested an Elmira attorney to bring an action in the courts to force his wife to turn over to his possession certain personal property which she is alleged to be keeping." His family had stood by him throughout his trial and prison term, but apparently, there had been little contact upon his release.

A *Gazette* reporter reached out to Mrs. Bundy but, "she declined to discuss the prospective action, though it was apparent that she was not surprised."

Frank E. Bundy died on January 3, 1935, after an extended illness. He was 75. (The voice of Frank's ghost was Rachel Dworkin, the archivist at the Chemung County Historical Museum)

About the authors and the TRUE STORIES book series....

Diane Janowski is the current Elmira City historian. She is also the editor of *New York History Review*, and was formerly the editor of the *Chemung Historical Journal*.

She has written many books about Elmira and Chemung County history, and co-authored the book *Images of America, The Chemung Valley* with Allen C. Smith.

James Hare is a retired teacher of American History and Government from the Elmira City School District. He is also a former mayor and councilman for the City of Elmira.

He co-authored the book *Images of America, Elmira* with former county historian J. Arthur Kieffer.

Hare and Janowski are freelance writers for the Elmira *Star-Gazette*. Since 2014, they each write monthly articles on the history of the city of Elmira, New York. This book is a selection of their articles.

www.ingramcontent.com/pod-product-compliance
Lightning Source LLC
LaVergne TN
LVHW011427080426
835512LV00005B/309